The Forgotten Governments

The Forgotten Governments
County Commissioners as Policy Makers

Vincent L. Marando and Robert D. Thomas

A Florida Atlantic University Book

The University Presses of Florida
Gainesville / 1977

84577

Library of Congress Cataloging in Publication Data

Marando, Vincent L.   1938–
  The forgotten governments.

  "A Florida Atlantic University book."
  Includes bibliographical references.
  1. County government—Florida. 2. County government—Georgia. I. Thomas, Robert D., 1940– joint
author. II. Title.
JS414.M37   352′.0073′0973   77–839
ISBN 0–8130–0569–8

Acknowledgments

WE have incurred a number of debts in the process of bringing this study to print. The study would not have been possible without the cooperation of Florida and Georgia county commissioners who answered our questionnaire. We appreciate the assistance of Hill R. Healan, executive director of the Association of County Commissioners of Georgia. During various stages of the project, we received financial support from the Office of Water Research and Technology, U.S. Department of the Interior, as authorized by the Water Resources Act of 1964 as amended, the Institute of Behavioral Research and the Institute of Government at the University of Georgia, and the College of Social Science at Florida Atlantic University.

We benefitted from the comments and counsel of a number of friends and colleagues. We should especially like to express appreciation to Keith G. Baker and Robert Sellers of the University of Georgia, John M. DeGrove of Florida Atlantic University, Thomas P. Murphy of the Federal Executive Institute, Charles Press of Michigan State University, Morris W. H. Collins of American University; each read the manuscript in whole or part and we profited by their suggestions. In addition, several former graduate students assisted us at one stage or another. Keith Hamm, Scott Reilly, James Herb, Ray Brown, and R. Wayne Boss assisted in collecting and compiling the data. Jane Thompson was especially helpful in editing the manuscript.

Those persons associated with the University Presses of Florida were of assistance to us, and Charles Tittle of the Florida Atlantic University publication committee was extremely helpful in providing critical review of the manuscript.

Contents

We dedicate this book to the women in our lives

Patty, Marianne, Shelley Anne, and Melissa Jane Marando
Anne, Tracy, and Laurie Thomas

Foreword

The Forgotten Governments: County Commissioners as Policy Makers
is a significant contribution to literature on county government. The
authors break new ground in the study of counties by adopting a
public policy framework for an assessment of county commissioners'
performances. Grounding their analysis in the cogent assumption that
public policy is the raw material with which government deals, they
adhere to this perspective throughout the study.

The approach taken is fundamentally empirical. They rely upon
data recording the perceptions of 253 county commissioners in Florida
and Georgia with respect to the problems facing their counties and
their attitudes about the responses counties should make in solving
the problems. Drawing primarily upon the results of a questionnaire
survey, the authors are careful to indicate where their analysis departs
from their data for the purposes of conjecture and hypothesis. Although their assessment pertains directly to counties in Florida and
Georgia, the approach and the discussion apply to counties in general; counties in other states are employed as bases for comparison
wherever appropriate.

In their approach, the authors have contributed two important
analytical tools to methodology in this area of study. For examining
the policies that counties have pursued, they have developed a framework that consists of three major variables: amount of urbanization,
degree of federal impact, and state in which the county is located.
The authors argue that these three variables determine to a large
extent how commissioners identify and respond to problems. They

also have developed a useful, fivefold classification scheme for policy analysis. Policies are classed according to their relationships to the areas of regulations, public utility services, social and remedial services, measures promoting economic development, and governmental-administrative measures. By means of such a system, the authors are able to assess which types of services are provided most frequently in response to such factors as urbanization and the reasons such choices are made. In short, their book represents the first serious attempt to classify county policies by employing some of the most recent theoretical literature on public policy and to determine where and why counties pursue some services more than others.

A number of significant conclusions are drawn in the study. Some shed new light on the dynamics of county government; others qualify a number of traditional assumptions; still others suggest areas for further research. Most important, they conclude that in many single metropolitan areas, counties are, in fact, the appropriate governmental units to deal with area problems because counties have broad territorial scope compared to other units. The authors cite some evidence indicating that many counties are assuming a more regional posture but conclude that only further research can determine whether they can be effective as regional governments.

The authors admit that the county must compete with the city as a target of research. Counties generally have been neglected as objects of analysis; much of what is known about them has been inferred from research on cities. As this survey indicates, county commissioners too often have regarded city government as a model, and some have assumed that counties should provide the same services as cities. One theme of this book is that the functioning and politics of the county must *not* be exclusively identified with those of the city. The significant differences between the two are assessed throughout the study, differences evolving primarily from the fact that the county, unlike the city, performs a dual function: it is simultaneously an administrative sub-unit of the state and a local government responding to local needs. Also, counties, which may include more than one jurisdiction, range geographically from the urban core through suburbs to rural areas, and they are faced necessarily with a broader array of demands than the basically urban city. This study indicates, then, that counties are sufficiently distinct to warrant caution in making generalizations about these two types of local governments.

The survey of commissioners and their policy roles is among the first to bring a high level of sophistication to the analysis of commissioner behavior, and it yields further conclusions that shed new light upon old assumptions. The analysis reveals that policy roles assumed by commissioners differ from what often is implied by the organizational charts that indicate a balanced commitment to administrative and legislative matters. Although they have the authority to perform both of these functions, the evidence indicates that they generally are selective in performing their duties and tend to engage far more in legislative than in administrative activities. Further, the examination of the decision-making styles of commissioners reveals that, outside of taxing, planning, and zoning, relatively few issues generate controversy: the general norm is uniformity in voting. The authors argue that the small size of commissions, the rural nature of many counties, and various social pressures can account for this tendency toward unified voting among commissioners.

Finally, a number of interesting findings regarding commissioner perceptions of county government emerge from the study. Generally, commissioners perceive their counties as genuine "local governments," which should provide all the services that citizens want, potentially including all that cities provide. The study indicates that counties, in fact, are tending to funnel into social services more of their resources from citizens and remedial legislation, under increasing pressures from citizens and higher levels of government to assume responsibility for these services. Commissioners consider a wide range of strategies as viable means for financing services, resisting only the property tax. Their attitudes toward controlling growth suggest that something approximating a state "culture" permeates county political activity. Attitudes toward growth vary between the two states: Florida commissioners are far more anti-growth than those in Georgia.

In conclusion, *The Forgotten Governments: County Commissioners as Policy Makers* presents a view of counties as developing organizations, continuing to perform their traditional role as administrative subdivisions of the state, while some of them also are evolving into corporate entities similar to municipal corporations. Counties are modernizing their structures and philosophies in response to the new demands being placed upon them as a result of increasing urbanization and population migrations.

THOMAS P. MURPHY
Director,
Federal Executive Institute

1

Counties: An Analytical Approach

FOR many citizens, county governments are enigmatic. On one hand, they stand as symbols of traditional local government. For a large segment of the American populace, county governments establish a link with the nation's rural heritage: "Although many counties are sufficiently populated to be classed as urban or semi-urban, a majority of them are primarily rural or small-town in composition and retain patterns of government that were created by an agrarian society. Counties provide civic links between rural citizens and the outside world. County government continues to reflect no little acceptance of the idea of performance by laymen or amateurs rather than by experts or professionals, unless politicians be classed as professionals."[1] On the other hand, county governments are more than remnants of the past. They perform a wide variety of necessary services for citizens, particularly those who live in the unincorporated areas.

County governments are the most territorially pervasive units of local government in the United States. With the exceptions of Connecticut, Rhode Island, and Alaska, the authority of county commissioners touches every geographic section of the country, though, of course, it varies widely from one geographic area to another. In the New England states, counties are especially weak because local power is in the hands of town councils; in the southern states, historically, counties have been and continue to be where local policy action exists. Counties may either share local power with cities or have greater

1. Daniel R. Grant and H. C. Nixon, *State and Local Government in America* (Boston: Allyn and Bacon, Inc., 1968), p. 413.

1

authority than cities. In fact, for many issues it is, to a larger extent, the county courthouse rather than city hall where local policy is largely effected in the South.[2] In the North, due to the historical concentration of population in urban areas, the "city hall" has been the locus of political power, but in the South this locus has centered around the "courthouse gang."

The county unit system, which entitled every county to a representative in the state legislature, enhanced the political power base of the "courthouse gang" in the South. For example, Fulton County (Atlanta), Georgia, was over three hundred times the size of Georgia's smallest county, yet each had one representative in the state legislature. Counties were given an added political advantage over other local units of government in determining the makeup of the state legislature. The unit system was particularly advantageous to rural counties: "Under the county unit system the influence of the most populous counties [was] greatly diminished and the power of the sparsely populated counties [was] tremendously enhanced."[3]

With the unit system, the county was the building block for constructing state political power. Thus, control of political power within the county had implications not only for local political power but also for state political power. The unit system insured a legislature attuned to county interests, one which would give added political advantages to the county in administering state programs as well as in administering state programs at the local level.

Following the United States Supreme Court's landmark decision on malapportionment of state legislatures in *Baker* v. *Carr* (and subsequent court decisions which institutionalized the one-man, one-vote principle), the courthouse gang's political power base at the state level was altered.[4] Rural counties lost representation in the legislature, while urban counties gained. Thomas R. Dye vividly illustrates this

2. Paul Wager, ed., *County Government across the Nation* (Chapel Hill: University of North Carolina Press, 1950).

3. Joseph L. Bernd, *Grass Roots Politics in Georgia* (Atlanta: Emory University Research Committee, 1960), p. 4.

4. *Baker* v. *Carr*, 369 U.S. 186 (1962) and *Gray* v. *Sanders*, 83 S. Ct. 801 (1963) are particularly important to mention because they prohibited further use of the county unit system of voting in statewide elections. *Westberry* v. *Sanders*, 84 S. Ct. 526 (1964) and *Reynolds* v. *Sims*, 84 S. Ct. 1362 (1964) are also very important because they decided that both houses of a state legislature must be apportioned on the basis of population. *Reynolds* v. *Sims*, for example, ruled against Alabama's attempt to base representation in its state senate on counties.

shift of political power as it occurred in Georgia: "Georgia's urban counties, which contain 53.3 per cent of the state's population, increased their representation in the Senate from 28.7 to 52.0 per cent and in the House from 24.9 to 48.8 per cent; rural counties, which contain 46.7 per cent of the state's population, decreased their representation from 71.3 to 47.9 per cent in the Senate and from 75.1 to 51.2 per cent in the House."[5] The impact of reapportionment, thus, has been to realign the political power base of counties, enhancing the power of urban counties and diminishing the power of rural counties.

Although, in the short run, reapportionment worked to the political advantage of city officials, its long-run effects have been to "increase the national role and political power of urban counties."[6] Since World War II, the United States has become increasingly a nation of suburbs which are outside city boundaries and under the jurisdiction of county commissioners. Murphy and Rehfuss contend that *Avery* v. *Midland County* was as significant as *Baker* v. *Carr* in bringing about this shift of local political power. *Avery* v. *Midland County* required "the reapportionment of county governmental bodies as well as state legislatures. In this case, 95 per cent of the county population lived in Midland City, but only one of the six commissioners was selected from that city. The others represented rural districts with populations between 400 and 800 persons. As a result of the reapportionment, Midland City residents were elected to all six positions. However, the long-term effect of the decision was to preclude central city politicians, who were controlling major urban counties, from denying proportionate representation to their burgeoning suburbs. In some cases, this eventually resulted in political control of the county by suburbanites."[7]

Even though their authorities vary widely from one state to another and from one geographic area to another, the decisions of county commissioners directly or indirectly affect citizens throughout the nation. County commissioners have some decision-making authority on almost every conceivable type of service performed at the local level: roads, public health facilities and services, libraries, law en-

5. Dye, *Politics in States and Communities*, 2d ed. (Englewood Cliffs, N.J.: Prentice-Hall, 1973), p. 132.
6. Thomas P. Murphy and John Rehfuss, *Urban Politics in the Suburban Era* (Homewood, Ill.: Dorsey Press, 1976), p. 161.
7. *Avery* v. *Midland County, Texas*, 88 S. Ct. 1114 (1968); Murphy and Rehfuss, p. 161.

forcement, solid waste management, schools and education, recreation, planning, zoning, and water management, as well as many others. Moreover, unlike cities and special districts, counties are involved not only in the delivery of local services but also in the administration of state services, such as elections, maintenance of records, and courts.

The services performed by county governments have undergone change throughout the history of the United States. Before the Revolution, colonial counties had characteristics of English parishes and served both ecclesiastic and civil purposes. Immediately following the Revolution, counties served mainly as administrative arms of state governments. Their role as administrative subdivisions of the state expanded the scope of their activities. New county organizations were established to collect taxes, subdivide and plot land, enforce laws, and engage in local administration of justice. Therefore, county governments expanded their organizations accordingly to include officers such as county treasurer, assessor, surveyor, sheriff, and prosecuting attorney.

THREE MAJOR INFLUENCES ON COUNTIES

As urbanization began to increase after the Civil War and continued even more intensely from World War I to the present, county services were expanded. The most important of these have been general governmental services. Counties, particularly those with urban characteristics, began taking on corporate structures to provide functions demanded by local populations. Thus, the principal state function that counties perform has been expanded with urbanization to include an additional role: counties as corporate entities.[8]

Urbanization makes a county commissioner's job more complicated and brings more socioeconomic complexity.[9] Citizens' demands

8. Herbert S. Duncombe, *County Government in America* (Washington: National Association of Counties Research Foundation, 1966), chap. 2.

9. We have used the Advisory Commission on Intergovernmental Relations' (ACIR) definitions. An urbanized county is defined in this study as one with a population of 100,000 and above. A non-urban county is defined as one with a population below 100,000. This figure was selected to make our definitions and analysis consistent with the definitions used by the National Association of Counties. Our definition of urban differs from that used by the Bureau of Census and by the Office of Management and Budget (OMB), which define urban in terms of Standard Metropolitan Statistical Areas (SMSAs). SMSA status is achieved when a county has a central city with a population of 50,000 or more or two cities with contiguous boundaries which are considered a single community with a combined population of 50,000 or more; the smaller of the two

on government are intensified by increased population size and density, more industrialization, and more resource needs (those variables generally considered to be concomitants of urbanization). Urbanization, in effect, intensifies both the number and the severity of public problems which confront county commissioners. In turn, it requires an increased level of governmental services and expenditures and a more involved role for commissioners in resolving conflicts among competing interests. Urbanization also complicates the governmental landscape because it not only intensifies demands for services and consensus building but also creates more problems of intergovernmental coordination. Urbanization breeds governmental complexity and puts county commissioners into problem-solving situations which require them (or county administrators) to associate with officials in other units of government, local, state, and federal.

Urbanization is not the only factor influencing county commissioners' responses to public problems.[10] A second important factor is the state. Counties, as indicated above, have always operated as administrative subdivisions of the state. Thus much of what counties do is directly affected by what the state requires them to do. More so than cities, counties have historical and substantive links to state government. Counties more than cities must look to the state for organizational, policy, and administrative guidance.

Although counties perform state-mandated services, they also have taken on new responsibilities. As a result, the traditional role of counties as state administrative arms has been expanded to encompass operating as municipal governments, albeit in some cases with difficulty. In many cases, for example, county commissioners must perform dual functions in responding to public problems. They must respond not only to problems arising out of the activities of governing,

---

must have a population of at least 15,000. The SMSA includes the county in which the city is located, and the county is the basic statistical unit (except for New England states, where the town is the basic statistical unit).

10. In the chapters that follow, we examine in some detail the factors of urbanization, state requirements, and federal programs as they influence county commissioners' responses to public problems. These three factors encompass the principal influences on policy makers. For example, the political science literature points to the impact of environmental factors (socioeconomic, demographic conditions), structural/organizational factors (reapportionment), and intergovernmental factors (impact of federal grants-in-aid and revenue sharing). We contend that urbanization, state requirements, and federal programs are the major variables which influence county commissioners' responses to public problems.

but also to problems arising from the contextual characteristics of their counties. Many of the problems which arise from the activities of governing come through the counties' role as administrators of state services. Many of their contextual problems are newly created as a result of their emerging role as corporate entities.

The two factors of state requirements and urbanization may also merge on some issues. For example, in growth management, counties are taking on new importance because they are perceived to be the optimal unit of local government (below the state level) with geographic expansiveness and political authority to deal with growth-related issues. Thus, growth management is becoming important in many counties because of urbanization, and many states which have established state laws for growth management (e.g., land use) are relying on the counties to administer state programs.

Federal programs are a third influence on county commissioners' responses to public problems. The transfer of federal funds through grants-in-aid and, more recently, through revenue-sharing funds is the major vehicle of federal influence. Federal grants-in-aid for both urban and rural programs have stimulated county involvement in new governmental activities. These programs have affected county allocation of funds to new services. Urban counties participate in a number of federal urban programs such as housing, construction of sewage treatment plants, and air and water pollution control. While the impact of federal urban programs has influenced county organization and the allocation of funds, other federal programs have also influenced counties and have expanded county services in both urban and rural areas. A partial list of these programs includes health and hospitals, welfare, roads and highways, parks and recreation, agricultural extension services, irrigation, drainage, and soil conservation.

Federal grant-in-aid programs have the same effect on counties as they have on other state and local recipients. For example, they have been shown to have political and administrative influences on recipients by altering political priorities of state and local officials by restricting the scope of available alternatives open to them;[11] altering state-local political relations by diminishing the need for local governmental dependency on state assistance in direct federal-local programs;[12] contributing to local governmental complexity and thus to

11. Deil S. Wright, *Federal Grants-in-Aid: Perspectives and Alternatives* (Washington: American Enterprise Institute, 1968), p. 8.
12. Robert D. Thomas, "Federal-Local Cooperation and Its Consequences

increased fragmentation of local political power;[13] contributing to fragmentation of local political forces at the state level;[14] creating a split between elected and administrative officials within the recipient government;[15] and reducing the political responsibility of elected officials.[16]

Although there is considerably less information on the effects of revenue sharing on county governmental responses to public problems, evidence is currently being gathered for a comprehensive study by the Brookings Institution.[17] The study's initial analysis establishes five conclusions (p. 128): (1) Per capita shared revenue is slightly less for metropolitan than non-metropolitan counties, is more for counties at each extreme of the ranges of population size and population density than for those between, and is considerably above average for counties with a high proportion of nonwhite population. (2) In relation to resident income, shared revenue increases markedly with decreased population size, decreased population density, and a higher proportion of nonwhite population. (3) In relation to local non-school taxes, local shared revenue increases strongly with decreased population size and decreased population density, but it does not vary consistently with the proportion of nonwhite population. (4) When separately examined, these patterns appear in the South as well as in

---

for State Level Policy Participation: Water Resources in Arizona," *Publius* 1, no. 2 (Winter 1972): 77–94.

13. U.S. Senate, Committee on Government Operations, Subcommittee on Intergovernmental Relations, *The Federal System as Seen by Federal Aid Officials* (Committee Print), 89th Cong., 1st sess., December 15, 1965.

14. Charles McKinley, "The Impact of American Federalism upon the Management of Land Resources," in *Federalism: Mature and Emergent*, ed. Arthur W. MacMahon (New York: Doubleday and Company, 1955), pp. 328–51.

15. Deil S. Wright and Richard L. McAnaw, *American State Administrators* (Iowa City: University of Iowa Department of Political Science and Institute of Public Affairs, Study Code and Marginal Tabulations, 1965); Basel J. F. Mott, "State Planning," in *The State and the Poor*, ed. Samuel H. Beer and Richard E. Barringer (Cambridge, Mass.: Winthrop, 1970), pp. 250–77; Robert D. Thomas, "Intergovernmental Coordination in the Implementation of National Air and Water Pollution Policies," in *Policy-Making in a Federal System*, ed. Charles O. Jones and Robert D. Thomas (Beverly Hills, Calif.: Sage Publications, Inc., 1976).

16. U.S. Congress, Commission on Intergovernmental Relations, *A Survey Report on the Impact of Federal Grants-in-Aid on the Structure and Functions of State and Local Governments* (Washington: U.S. Government Printing Office, 1955).

17. Richard P. Nathan, Allen D. Manvel, Susannah E. Calkins, and Associates, *Monitoring Revenue Sharing* (Washington: The Brookings Institution, 1975).

other parts of the country. (5) The county-area variations can be traced in large part to differences in income level. Mainly as they affect the local-allocation stage of the distribution formula, these differences work to the severe disadvantage of the most populous and densely settled county areas.

The literature on counties is scanty. Most county studies do not bring to bear contemporary concepts in political science and advances in methodology. The bulk of these studies is simply "not systematic, behavioral, or theoretical." John C. Bollens characterizes the literature on counties as descriptive and prescriptive, couched in legalistic, institutional frameworks, scattered throughout a wide range of publications, and touching on variegated topics.[18] But there have been exceptions, particularly in recent years, for example, Edward Sofen's interesting and trend-setting analysis of Miami-Metro consolidation, Thomas P. Murphy's case study of Jackson County, Missouri, as an urban county in transition in a major metropolitan area, Susan Torrence's *Grass Roots Government*, and Thomas Murphy and John Rehfuss' *Urban Politics in the Suburban Era*.[19]

In this study, we want to add to the research on county governments by taking an approach which differs significantly from the traditional studies referred to by Bollens. Our approach also differs from the more recent, more systematic analyses of counties, not because we think these studies are not important contributions but because we feel there is a need for an analysis broader than cases of one county. This book is about county commissioners and their counties. Principally from the perspective of the county commissioner, we describe and analyze the counties' responses to public problems. We place county commissioners and their counties in a different framework than does the traditional literature, establishing one which focuses on the men and women who govern counties. We are not concerned with how counties ought to respond to public problems but with how they do, in fact, respond, given the configuration of problems confronting them.

In each chapter, we examine specific questions dealing with the

18. Bollens, *American County Government* (Beverly Hills, Calif.: Sage Publications, Inc., 1969), pp. 12–13, 15–17.

19. Sofen, *The Miami Metropolitan Experiment* (Bloomington: Indiana University Press, 1963); Murphy, *Metropolitics and the Urban County* (Washington: Washington National Press, 1970); Torrence, *Grass Roots Government: The County in American Politics* (Washington: Robert B. Luce, Inc., 1974); Murphy and Rehfuss, see p. 3n6.

factors which influence county commissioners' responses to public problems: the organizational context within which commissioners must operate in responding to such problems; an assessment of the priorities commissioners place on selected problems; an analysis of commissioners' perceptions of governmental responsibilities (their own and those of other levels of government, local, state, and federal) on selected problems; the policy roles commissioners perform, administrative and/or legislative, and their decision-making processes; and an assessment of commissioners' performances in delivering services and of the operation of commissions as corporate entities.

Our approach is different from those of recent studies in that our focus is more broadly based. While our analysis relies principally, although not exclusively, on attitudinal data of county commissioners in Florida and Georgia, we have attempted to broaden the scope of our knowledge about counties beyond case studies of individual counties. It is true that such studies bring rich detail to an understanding of counties, but we must be careful how we generalize from them. We are aware of similar limitations in a comparative two-state study of counties, but our study involves 226 units of local government (67 counties in Florida and 159 counties in Georgia). Thus, what we may sacrifice in detail, we attempt to make up for in the breadth of the study.

How adequately do the Florida and Georgia counties represent "all" counties in the United States? They illustrate many basic characteristics of counties throughout the nation (though, of course, in varying degrees). These characteristics include the organization of counties, the scope of problems that confront county commissioners, the impact of urbanization, the impact of the American federal system (i.e., the sharing or non-sharing of governmental responsibility in dealing with problems), decisional and policy roles, demands for services, and the ways in which these demands require county commissioners not only to assume their traditional activities but also to expand their activities to new endeavors.

What are the characteristics of the typical county commissioner in Florida and Georgia? The commissioner is usually a male living in a small town or a suburb of the county's largest city. If he governs in a metropolitan county, he lives either in the city or in the suburbs. Usually he has lived in the county he presently serves almost all his life. He was either born in that county or, having been born in the state, moved to that county from another section of the state. A

Georgia county commissioner is more likely than a Florida commissioner to have been born in the county or in another section of the state. He is a registered Democrat, although occasionally a Florida commissioner is a Republican. Whether from Florida or Georgia, he is an amateur politician, generally never having held another public office and with almost no ambitions to run for other political offices. If he does, it is for another local administrative or elective office. Occasionally, he might consider a state office, but he has absolutely no interest in a national office. (See Appendix A for a detailed data profile of Florida and Georgia county commissioners.)

RESPONDING TO PUBLIC PROBLEMS: A FRAMEWORK

There are a number of factors involved in public officials' responses to public problems. The raw material with which government deals is public problems.[20] As a rule it is difficult to define generally a single, root problem which makes up a public problem. Several examples will illustrate this. Crime is perceived to be a variety of subproblems, ranging from procedural methods to prevent or deal with crime (e.g., law enforcement, judicial reform, harsher penalties) to substantive causes of crime (e.g., unemployment, education, drugs, poverty). Water problems involve both quantity—having an adequate water supply for domestic, industrial, and agricultural purposes—and quality—controlling water pollution to sustain fish and wildlife, as well as human life.

The complexity of the American system of government also complicates governmental responses. From the beginning of the Republic, we have established diverse, fragmented authorities which are located in various units and levels of government. In many cases, as a result, policy solutions are devised as much, if not more, to disperse governmental authority and protect the integrity of the way the system operates as to solve public problems.

The oversimplified model in Figure 1 shows governmental procedures being established to respond to substantive public problems. The theoretical basis of government in the United States was drawn from the social-contract theorists, particularly John Locke. Locke, standing in the tradition of Hobbes, Spinoza, and Rousseau, saw government as necessary to deal with problems that evolved out of

20. See the definition of a public problem offered by Charles O. Jones, *An Introduction to the Study of Public Policy* (Belmont, Calif.: Wadsworth, 1970).

societal conflicts. He did not agree, however, with the major thrust of much of this writing, that without government there would be societal chaos. In order to provide a basis for dissolving government, Locke theorized that a society could exist peaceably without government. Nonetheless, at the basis of governmental action are societal problems. Problems to which county commissioners must respond arise from three sources: the contextual characteristics of their governing jurisdictions (i.e., the socioeconomic, demographic, and political problems within their county); the legal, organizational, and structural constraints which define the boundaries of their authority and jurisdiction; and the numerous political compromises which have been established in attempting to respond to these two groups of problems. Therefore, to analyze how governments (in this case, county governments) respond to public problems, we need to understand the socioeconomic and demographic impacts of commissioners' responses to public problems, the scope of their authorities, how they use their authorities (decisional styles and policy roles utilized), and their interactions with other units and levels of government in sharing responsibilities.

To set up our analysis of how county commissioners respond to public problems, we have adopted a systems frame of reference. We deal with a selected range of public problems and analyze the commissioners' perceptions of these problems and their responsibilities for dealing with them. We focus on particular types of decision-making and policy roles, and we deal with selected service deliveries.

A focus on issues.—Since David Easton's seminal work,[21] students of public policy have moved from an institutional focus to attempt to assess the impact of socioeconomic and political forces on policy outputs[22] and to determine the influence of public policies on political processes.[23]

Policy scholars have utilized various ways of thinking about public issues. Some have emphasized the processes by which policies are

---

21. Easton, *A System Analysis of Political Life* (New York: John Wiley and Sons, 1965).

22. In the past decade or so, this literature has become voluminous. For an excellent review of this literature as well as other state and local policy studies, see Charles O. Jones, "State and Local Public Policy Analysis: A Review of Progress," in *Political Science and State and Local Government* (Washington: American Political Science Association, 1973), pp. 27–54.

23. See, for example, Theodore Lowi, *The End of Liberalism* (New York: Norton, 1969).

Fig. 1. Sequence of governmental responses to public problems

Initial governmental response   New problems, both substantive and procedural

Substantive public problem (economic, social)	→	Procedures established to respond (policy processes, authorities, division of responsibilities)	→	Public policy → response → public policy → response
			→	Public policy → response → public policy → response
			→	Public policy → response → public policy → response

Fig. 2. County commissioners' responses to public problems

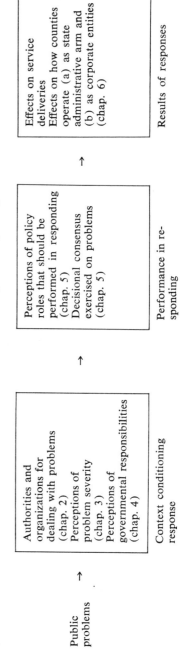

Public problems → [Authorities and organizations for dealing with problems (chap. 2); Perceptions of problem severity (chap. 3); Perceptions of governmental responsibilities (chap. 4)] → [Perceptions of policy roles that should be performed in responding (chap. 5); Decisional consensus exercised on problems (chap. 5)] → [Effects on service deliveries; Effects on how counties operate (a) as state administrative arm and (b) as corporate entities (chap. 6)]

Context conditioning response   Performance in responding   Results of responses developed. Such an emphasis on these processes has been criticized for being apart from any specific policy or issue, for developing generalizations about groups but giving "little attention to policies or the policy choices that the groups favor or oppose," for treating individuals who participate in the process as a "type or as a statistic or as a ghostlike entity that plays a role rather than as a flesh-and-blood human being who is purposive and who reasons and argues in supporting or opposing a specific line of action." These studies, according to Vernon Van Dyke, teach us "astoundingly little about substantive aspects of [public issues]. There is no attempt to inform the reader of different perceptions of issues, different lines of reasoning concerning it, different prescriptions for its solution, and different consequences that are likely to follow different choices. The focus is on the general and enduring features of the process, not on the transient factors relating to mortal persons and their thoughts about a policy problem."[24]

In recent years there has been completed a spate of policy studies which attempt to broaden our understanding of how policies are developed to respond to public problems.[25] One of the major contributions of these studies has been to direct our attention away from the institutional confines of processes to the impact of socioeconomic and political factors and their influence on policy outputs. Less voluminous, but nonetheless important, have been attempts to assess how policies influence political processes. The groundwork for this approach was laid by Theodore Lowi's work. Charles O. Jones' analyses of public policy have also led to insights into the impact of public problems on political processes. It is Jones' contention, and he has shown this to be so empirically, that public problems are "the grist for the policy makers' mill." He argues that we should focus on public problems and see how they are handled by government. This requires a concern for substantive public problems and cross-institutional relationships (i.e., legislative-executive-administrative relations and intergovernmental relations).[26]

A primary dimension in analyzing governmental responses to public problems is public officials' perceptions. As Jones points out, "The

24. Van Dyke, "Process and Policy as Focal Concepts in Political Research," in *Political Science and Public Policy*, ed. Austin Ranney (Chicago: Markham Publishing Co., 1968), pp. 24, 25.

25. See note 22.

26. Theodore Lowi, "American Business, Public Policy, Case-Studies, and Political Theory," *World Politics* 16 (July 1964): 677–715; Jones, *Introduction to the Study of Public Policy* and "State and Local Public Policy Analysis."

crucial variable in explaining behavior is frequently not how things actually are but rather how they are perceived."[27] It is from examination of commissioners' perceptions that we pursue assessment of county government. As will be explained, we concentrate on the commissioners' perceptions of a selected number of public problems, of their own and other officials' responsibilities for handling and attempting to solve problems, and of their actions on problems, i.e., services needed.

Taking our frame of reference from recent policy studies, we begin our analysis of county commissioners and their counties with an assessment of the context of responses to problems, that is, those factors which operate to condition how responses are made. Numerous factors, of course, influence commissioners' responses. As shown in Figure 2, we concentrate on three broad factors: the authoritative and organizational context, the problem context, and the intergovernmental context.

The first of these factors, the authoritative and organizational context within which commissioners must operate, establishes the legal boundaries of their responses to problems. Certain characteristics of county authorities and organization place limitations on commissioners' abilities to respond. Thus the existence of independent elected county officials (sheriff, tax assessor) fragments commissioners' authorities to govern their counties. Restrictions and limitations on counties' taxing authority imposed by state legislatures limit their ability to respond. For example, counties in Florida and Georgia are not allowed to raise revenue through income or sales taxes; this legal restriction severely limits their ability to raise revenue for solving public problems. On the other hand, authority and organizational characteristics can enhance commissioners' abilities to respond. For instance, home rule authority may allow counties to operate as independent corporate entities. That is, by utilizing home rule authority, counties can respond to the demands of residents without having to obtain specific authority from the state. In addition, organizational arrangements which professionalize county administration (e.g., a county executive officer) may enhance commissioners' abilities to respond.

The second dimension of the context of commissioners' responses deals with the problems that confront county commissioners. Which

27. Jones, *Introduction*, p. 35.

are most pressing? How does the problem context for commissioners from urban areas differ from that of non-urban commissioners? To assess the problem context of county commissioners, we deal with commissioners' perceptions of the severity of a selected list of public problems. We assume that the problems confronting county commissioners are influenced in large measure by the commissioners' cognitive assessment of which are severe and which are not. As a theoretical premise, perception of problem severity indicates not only substantive concerns of commissioners (e.g., inadequate roads, overcrowded schools, pollution, etc.) but also political considerations, for while he may feel two problems are equally severe from the standpoint of substantive concerns, he may elevate one to a higher priority due to interest-group pressures and public opinion.

The third dimension in Figure 2 which makes up the context of commissioners' responses is the responsibilities and authorities of other units and levels of government. The American federal system was established and has evolved as a method of governing to achieve unity in a heterogeneous society. Its purpose was and is to integrate a diverse, highly fragmented society in order to find consensus among its people and to maintain political stability through dispersion of authority. As county commissioners operate within these confines, they must share governmental responsibilities with officials from state and national governments, as well as from other local governments, which will influence how commissioners respond to problems. For example, county residents may demand an increased water supply, but the facilities for obtaining and distributing water are often controlled by cities. Therefore, commissioners either must cooperate with city officials for water supplies or invest large amounts of capital in building county water facilities. As with problem severity, we analyze commissioners' perceptions of their responsibilities as well as the responsibilities of other units and levels of government on selected problems.

Performance in responding to problems.—The second part of our analysis deals with the commissioners' performances in responding to problems. In assessing performance, we deal with two major ingredients, policy roles and decisional consensus. According to much of the literature on county government, the principal job of commissioners is the administration, or at least the overseeing, of county services; however, there is no assessment of the actual job activities performed by commissioners. County commissioners are the major policy makers within counties. What policy functions do they perform? The way in which commissioners approach their policy roles will be affected by the problems they confront. For example, an urban commissioner may of necessity be more a legislator than an administrator, whereas a rural (or non-urban) commissioner may assume an active role in administering county functions.

Another important factor in assessing commissioners' performances in responding to problems is decisional consensus. County commissioners perform as committees. Each commissioner is equal insofar as his vote is concerned. The size of the commissions (typically five, but varying in Florida and Georgia from one to eleven members) makes decisional consensus an integral part of commissioners' performance in responding to public problems. Our concern is with decisional consensus (agreement-disagreement) on selected problems. What are the characteristics of decisional consensus? Does the size of the commission make a difference? Does decisional consensus vary by type of county (urban or non-urban)?

Results of responses.—As shown in Figure 2, the third dimension of our analysis deals with the results of county governmental responses to public problems. As indicated, the activities of government evolve out of both responses to substantive problems and the procedural activities of government. In assessing the results of county responses (e.g., in service deliveries), we must consider counties as a hybrid form of local government. For example, counties operating as administrative subdivisions of the state are "required" to deliver certain services, such as welfare, roads, and law enforcement. Therefore, their responses on these activities are defined outside the county chambers. On the other hand, counties operating as corporate entities are able to define what problems they will respond to and how. What are the commissioners' attitudes about providing services that are not "required" by the state?

Many generalizations about county governments come from research on city governments. Therefore, in examining results of county government responses, we want not only to look at how counties function as state administrative subdivisions and as corporate entities but also to compare counties to cities.

2

County Authorities and Organizations

COUNTY governments have a wide variety of authorities and organizational structures, which vary from state to state and, within states, from county to county. A principal organizational characteristic of counties is that commissioners and independent administrative officials are separately elected and have authority to operate in a semi-autonomous fashion. Broadly speaking, county organizational structures range from the merging of legislative and administrative authority in a single body to the distribution of these governmental functions to separate branches of county government.[1]

There are three basic forms of county organization: the commission form, the county-manager form, and the council–elected-executive form. Each of these forms was shaped by a multitude of factors, and each has an impact on how commissioners resolve public problems. Of the 226 counties in Florida and Georgia, 167 are represented by commissions; this form combines both the legislative and administrative functions in a single body. Of the 226 counties, 58 have an appointed-county-manager structure, an arrangement which delegates the legislative function to the elected commission and the supervision of administration to the appointed manager. Two counties in Florida and one in Georgia have the council–elected-executive form, a gov-

1. All county commissioners can enact ordinances (i.e., legislate) as well as supervise administrators; however, the distinction we are making between legislative and administrative functions is that in some counties, particularly rural counties, commissioners not only legislate but actually administer county activities.

ernmental structure which represents the full separation of powers between the commission and the manager (chief executive). This is, of course, the model of separation of powers which is characteristic of the national government. Under this system the commission performs the legislative function, and the elected executive implements policies and is responsible for administration.

City-county consolidation is a new organizational form of county government which is gaining credence in some states across the nation. Two counties in Florida (Jacksonville-Duval and Miami-Dade) and one in Georgia (Columbus-Muscogee) have a consolidated city-county structure.

The organizational structure of counties has not been rigid and impervious to change. Rather, county legislative and administrative authorities have evolved in response to changing needs and demands. New administrative units have been created. Counties in all areas of Florida and Georgia are expanding their authorities. In addition, new responsibilities are being placed on counties by both the state and national governments.

The demands affecting county organization arise primarily from three sources. The first is the state, which is the "creator" of counties. As states' roles and functions have expanded, evidenced by their providing increased services, the impact has influenced the organization and functions of counties. It is the county which administers many of the expanded services for the state, such as highway and criminal justice programs. The second source, increased federal grant programs, has stimulated larger and more complicated county organizations. One example of the impact of federal grants is the Law Enforcement Assistance Administration (LEAA), which has stimulated counties to develop larger public safety departments. (LEAA funds have allowed sheriffs' departments to hire more officers and to buy more equipment.) Further, federal grants have encouraged the creation of new county-wide organizations, such as pollution agencies.[2] The third source is residents who expect counties to serve as corporate local governments capable of resolving many public problems. As the organization of municipal corporations has become larger and more complex in response to the demands of residents, the organiza-

2. New organizations created as a response to federal programs may be multi-county in scope. For example, a newly created Economic Growth District in Kansas, encompassing a fourteen-county area, recently became eligible for federal financial assistance.

tion of counties has also been affected. The development of counties into local corporate governments has been accelerated by federal programs, many of which (such as health and hospitals) have encouraged and enabled counties to perform corporate functions.

Federal grant stimulation, together with the increased dual purposes of counties acting as state subdivisions as well as local corporate governments, has a direct effect on county organization and problem solving by commissioners. In this chapter, we approach county organization by first discussing the changing roles and demands being placed upon counties. Next we present in detail an approach for analyzing the basic characteristics of all counties in Florida and Georgia by examining counties both as territorial units and as corporate units. Finally, the major organizational structures of Florida and Georgia counties are examined and discussed.

COUNTIES: ORGANIZATIONS UNDER CHANGE

Former Georgia Governor Carl E. Sanders stated that "historically, county governments are the proper administrative agents, and it is through them, in substantial measure, that state programs are translated into reality and brought directly to the people. Counties are the traditional right arm of the State Government."[3] In that counties historically have been considered administrative and service branches of the state, it was logical for state governments to specify how county governing bodies should be structured.[4] Most assessments of county government stress the fact that shortly after the Revolutionary War, counties were created as administrative subdivisions of the state and are a major mechanism through which state programs and services are delivered to local citizenry. The organization of counties, thus, is established by the state constitution or by legislative statutes. But in many states, authority to alter county organization is delegated to the localities themselves. The localities' authority falls into two categories: states where the county governing board may change the organizational structure through resolution and states where a voter referendum is required for any change in form.[5]

3. Sanders, "The Traditional Right Arm of the State," *Georgia County Government Magazine*, May 1965, pp. 12–13.

4. Torrence, *Grass Roots Government: The County in American Politics*, p. 7.

5. Florence Zeller, "Counties Seek Flexibility through Structural Changes,"

In Table 1, we summarize state delegation of authority to counties for altering county organizational structures. The states listed in group A have no optional organizational authority delegated at the local level. In group B, states grant to localities the authority to alter organizations only through voter referendum. In the states listed in group C, organizational structures can be changed by resolution of the county board. Both Florida and Georgia are in group B. It has been the trend for an increasing number of states to grant to localities expanded options and less stringent political requirements, such as altering county structures by commission resolution rather than by voter referendum.

The states' delegation of increased authority to counties is a relatively recent phenomenon of the last several decades. Historically, the creation of counties as state subdivisions had its roots in Anglo-Saxon England. The shire was the administrative subdivision and was the model used for creating county government in the United States. The basic administrative functions performed in England (such as judicial, police, public works) were also assigned to counties in the United States. Using the British model, the American colonists wrote state constitutions which conceived of counties as extensions of state government at the local level. In state constitutions prior to the late 1800s, the status of counties as an arm of state government continued.[6]

The role of the county as an administrative subdivision of the state is better understood if viewed in relation to the increasing scope of state services to be administered. Until the Depression of the 1930s, state governments provided relatively few services. Before the Depression, the major county activities (e.g., tax assessment and collection, law enforcement [sheriff], judicial administration, and the construction and maintenance of roads and bridges) were centered around administering state programs. The growth of state service activities is dramatically illustrated by the increase of state revenues from $200 million in 1902 to $89 billion in 1970, representing a 445-fold increase.[7] In the early 1900s, states did not provide many services, and counties were the administrative mechanism for few services. As the

New County Times, January 28, 1974 (Washington: National Association of County Offices), p. 5.

6. Duncombe, *County Government in America*, pp. 18, 23.

7. U.S. Bureau of the Census, *Historical Statistics of the United States* (Washington: U.S. Government Printing Office, 1960), p. 727. Updated.

United States became more urbanized following World War II, the need for physical and social programs grew, and county general services expanded accordingly.

In several ways, counties, particularly those in urban areas, are undergoing change from the exclusive role of state administrative subdivisions. Organizationally, counties are increasingly being transformed into local governments as well as administrative subdivisions of the state. A local government, as distinct from a state sub-unit, is

TABLE 1
STATE DELEGATION OF AUTHORITY TO COUNTIES FOR
ALTERING ORGANIZATIONAL STRUCTURES

A. In these 17 states, counties must operate under the commission (or a very weak executive-commission) form of government. In a few cases, special state legislation can be sought for individual county changes.

Alabama	Kentucky	Oklahoma
Arkansas	Maine	Texas
Delaware	Massachusetts	Vermont
Idaho	Mississippi	West Virginia
Iowa	Nebraska	Wyoming
Kansas	New Hampshire	

B. In these 18 states, any alternative plan must be put to a voter referendum, either through adoption of a charter or a special question on the proposed change in form.

Colorado	Missouri	Oregon
Florida	Montana	Pennsylvania
Georgia	New Jersey	South Dakota
Hawaii	New York	Tennessee
Illinois	North Dakota	Utah
Louisiana	Ohio	Washington

C. In these 13 states, the county governing board may adopt some alternative to the commission plan of government simply by resolution. In a few cases, the board may put the question to the voters if it so resolves. In one case (S.C.), voter approval is required for two of the five optional forms. In some cases, no optional forms are specifically prescribed. In these instances, administrators have been hired on the basis of constitutional authority to employ whatever officers are deemed necessary to carry out duties of the governing board.

Alaska	Michigan	North Carolina
Arizona	Minnesota	South Carolina
California	Nevada	Virginia
Indiana	New Mexico	Wisconsin
Maryland		

SOURCE: Adapted from data presented in *New County Times*, January 28, 1974, p. 6.

created and organized in response to the particular needs of local populations. Because the needs of local populations may differ throughout a state, counties' responses to the requirements of local populations may vary throughout a state. Counties are coming to resemble locally responsive corporate governments, namely municipalities.

There are several reasons for the transformation of counties into local governments as well as state administrative sub-units. Citizens are demanding more services from all levels of government, especially counties. The major population movement in urban areas from cities to suburbs has had a profound impact upon counties. Most population growth in the United States during the last three decades has been suburban growth.[8] The suburban population of the United States (persons living in metropolitan areas but outside the central city) grew 36.0 per cent during the 1960s, while the central cities grew only 8.4 per cent. In addition, much of this 8.4 per cent city growth was the result of boundary changes, such as annexation, rather than population migration to cities. Today, suburbanites, constituting 36.5 per cent, outnumber both central-city residents with 31.9 per cent and rural residents with 32.9 per cent of the American population.[9] This trend of population shift to suburban areas will continue unabated in the seventies. Overall, cities and rural areas have accounted for a relatively small portion of growth, and many cities and rural areas have lost population during this period.

This population movement away from major cities and into suburban towns and unincorporated areas has increased the need for county governments to provide "city-type" services in the unincorporated suburban areas as well as to supplement the services provided by small suburban jurisdictions. Frequently, these jurisdictions must contract with counties for services because they do not have the fiscal or organizational capacity to provide the services themselves. For example, a suburban community, such as Watkinsville, Georgia (population 1,800), contracts with Oconee County (population 10,000) to have police patrol within the city limits.

In Georgia and Florida, as well as in other states, counties are the only general-purpose suburban governments. A majority of the sub-

8. See Alan K. Campbell, *The States and the Urban Crisis* (Englewood Cliffs, N.J.: Prentice-Hall, Inc., 1970), and Murphy and Rehfuss, *Urban Politics in the Suburban Era*, pp. 9–12.
9. U.S. Bureau of the Census, *1970 Census of Population*, P–C(P3)–3 (Washington: U.S. Government Printing Office, 1971).

urban population in the two states lives in unincorporated county areas. The central cities of Florida and Georgia are not surrounded by suburban municipalities to the same extent as are cities in the Northeast, West, and Midwest. Therefore, most suburbanites in Florida and Georgia must rely upon county government to provide services that they might normally expect to receive from cities. If residents in Florida and Georgia want police protection, roads, water, sewers, or any other services commonly provided by suburban municipalities in other regions of the nation, they must request them from counties.

Counties are being confronted by more localized requests and demands from residents. Counties were created to provide state services to all local areas, regardless of the specialized desires of residents, not specifically to meet localized demands which may differ from place to place (e.g., some localities may want quality libraries while other areas may want no libraries at all). Yet all counties are to varying degrees responsive to local problems, in addition to providing state services at the local level. The functioning of counties as corporate entities is not consistent with the legal principle of the constitutional supremacy of states. A decision by the Ohio Supreme Court, representative of the commonly accepted view of the role of counties, made the distinction between a city (created for convenience of the locality) and a quasi-municipal corporation, such as a county, created with a view to the policy of the state at large.[10] Thus, the predominant view that counties are departments of the state did not prohibit them from evolving into local governments.

Since county commissioners must administer state functions and also act in a policy-making capacity as local governors, they are subjected to two sets of demands. Commissioners must respond to all the administrative requirements of the states. They are directed by state statutes, and often by constitutional requirements as well, to provide certain state functions within their jurisdiction. Further, the structure of counties is mandated by the state and applies to all counties.

Constitutional amendments or legislated statutes applying to a single county are necessary to alter the structure and organization of county government. For example, counties in Florida and Georgia are required to have independently elected administrative officers

10. Duncombe, *County Government*, chaps. 1, 2.

such as the sheriff and tax assessor. These administrative officers are elected separately from the commissioners and are responsible for the administration of certain state functions that counties provide. The fact that these administrators are not appointed by the commissioners but elected by the citizens gives them a greater degree of independence in performing the duties of their offices.

Organizationally, county structure resembles a collection of relatively independent administrators as well as a single policy-making body in the form of the county commission. This organizational form is contrary to what public administrators suggest as a "modern" structure: a single policy-making body which appoints the administrators.[11] This "modern" structure would then assign policy-making and administration functions to the commission and appointed administrators, respectively.

Counties administering state programs are also limited in the options open to them for raising revenues. Counties must raise revenues in accordance with state statutes, which restrict the latitude of the types and amounts of taxes that can be generated. Counties as well as cities and special districts are prohibited from raising revenues through an income tax or sales tax. Counties in Florida and Georgia, therefore, rely heavily upon the property tax, user charges, and state aid in carrying out their functions. These relatively narrow resource options influence the scope and flexibility of county organizations in performing services. Counties are thus forced to seek alternative forms of resources available to them, such as fee charges and federal aid. These alternative resources have an impact on the type of services counties will provide. For example, fee charges are attached to a specific function (e.g., recreation). Also, categorical grants-in-aid are attached to a specific function, such as planning or law enforcement. These resource alternatives offer counties a range of options that are narrow, on the one hand (e.g., fees), and whose objectives are being defined outside county jurisdiction on the other (e.g., federal grants).

One means of permitting counties more flexibility in meeting the needs of modern urban and suburban society is through home rule charters. Like city charters, these charters are permanent grants of power to counties. In effect, they designate counties as the units to provide city-type services in large urban areas. Charles R. Adrian defines home rule as "the power granted to local units of government

11. James M. Banovetz, *Managing the Modern City* (Washington: International City Management Association, 1971).

to frame, adopt, and amend charters for their government and to exercise powers of local self-government subject to the constitution and general laws of the state." Murphy and Rehfuss sum up the effects of home rule on financing services by indicating that "Home rule is one means of giving suburban county governments authority commensurate with their responsibilities—it gives them increased financial flexibility."[12]

The county as "local government" has been further reinforced by the federal government in its general revenue-sharing program.[13] Both counties and cities have been designated to receive federal revenue-sharing funds. This designation is due in part to recognition by Congress of the county as a viable unit of local government, organizationally capable of providing a wide range of services that do not neatly fit the boundaries of cities. The county's receipt of revenue-sharing funds recognizes its corporate governmental status and contributes further to the county's increased corporate development. If the county were viewed by Congress as strictly an administrative sub-unit of the state, the revenue-sharing funds would logically have been allocated to the states. The states, at their exclusive discretion, might then have administratively dispersed revenue-sharing funds through counties, or they might have by-passed counties.

Commissioners in their capacity as "local governors" are subjected to many of the same pressures as are city councilmen. Citizens often turn to county government when they want police and fire protection, water, sewers, recreational facilities, or a host of other city-type services. As indicated, counties are the local government for more than half of the Florida and Georgia population—residents who do not live in cities. The county commissioners are the only local governors with authority to respond to service demands of residents in unincorporated areas. Generally, the responsiveness of counties as local governments is increasing in all areas of Florida and Georgia, although the extent to which counties function as local government and respond to citizen demands varies. Counties in the urban areas are much more responsive as local governments to residents' service needs than are the more rural counties. Residents of urban areas demand

12. Adrian, *State and Local Government* (New York: McGraw-Hill, 1960), pp. 122–24; Murphy and Rehfuss, *Urban Politics in the Suburban Era*, p. 149.
13. For a comprehensive analysis of the legislative action preceding passage and the final form of PL 92–512 (general revenue sharing), see "Congress Clears Nixon's Revenue-Sharing Plan," *Congressional Quarterly Almanac* (Washington: Congressional Quarterly, Inc., 1972), pp. 636–52.

more services than rural residents; to suburban residents, the county
is their suburb.

The increasing role of counties as local governments and state
administrative sub-units provides a double set of policy boundaries within which commissioners function. They function in organizations that are confronted with a state-local blend of administrative
tasks and policy requests. County government is increasingly functioning as a local government while simultaneously performing state
administrative functions, which in themselves are expanding. Higher
standards and increased state regulations are being applied to virtually
all state programs delivered through the counties. For instance, the
administration of state road or law enforcement programs attests to
the increase in standards of performance of service delivery at the
county level. The county must conform to state requirements for environmental impact statements for all new county road construction.

TERRITORIAL SCOPE

In territorial scope, there are a number of differences between counties and cities. To begin with, counties are territorially pervasive: in
most states (including Florida and Georgia), all land area, whether
heavily or sparsely populated, falls under the jurisdiction of a county
government.[14] Hence, counties as territorial units encompass the
entire state. Counties have within their boundaries cities, suburbs,
and rural areas. Cities are by definition urban. Second, unlike cities,
counties are not voluntarily created governments, created solely to
meet the needs of populated areas. Instead, counties are created by
the state and are governmentally applicable to all the inhabitants of
the area they cover. In fact, there does not have to be a relationship
between population concentrations and the location of county governments. Counties serve rural populations which, in comparison to
urban populations, require limited governmental services. Generally
speaking, this means that rural residents require fewer complex
county organizational structures to deliver services than do urban
populations.[15]

14. Alaska is the exception to the rule of territorial pervasiveness of counties. The sparsely settled winter lands of Alaska are not organized into local
governmental units, nor are Connecticut and Rhode Island organized into
counties.
15. York Willbern, *The Withering Away of the City* (Bloomington: Indiana
University Press, 1964), pp. 24, 35, and chap. 2.

By contrast, cities are corporate local governmental structures, and are not territorially inclusive. Residents may or may not live within a city. Obviously, cities as corporate governments are designed for the needs of urban populations. Although cities are, like counties, creatures of the state, they are essentially formed through the initiative of local residents to perform (within state limits) those activities the local populace desires. Residents of urban areas incorporate into cities to raise revenue to provide those services they desire in addition to those the state provides to all its residents, urban and rural.

This distinction between counties and cities is further evidenced by the way the states relate to them. State constitutions and laws say relatively little about the organization of cities, on the theory that these units were established mainly to meet the demands of local residents who should therefore decide how to structure their own government.[16] This contrasts, as we shall see shortly, with county organizations which receive considerably more attention from the states.

The significance of counties as territorial local governments and cities as corporations is dramatized as populations suburbanize. When the pattern of population settlement changes in relationship to the existence of local governments, many suburbanites may no longer live in cities. Often, existing cities cannot meet the needs of suburban residents requesting local governmental services. Generally, city residence is required for obtaining all city services.[17] When urban or suburban residents in unincorporated areas want services, the county is then called on to function as a corporate local government and to provide services that cities normally provide.

The impact of the "fit" between counties as territorial and corporate local governments has consequences for how and what demands are made upon counties. Counties are often the only local governments that have sufficient territorial scope to encompass metropolitan areas, that is, a county's jurisdiction includes both cities and unincorporated suburban fringes. Cities, suburbs, and urbanizing rural areas are often all located within a single county. Often, public problems that are generated in urban areas overlap existing city govern-

16. Torrence, *Grass Roots Government*, p. 7.
17. There are instances when suburbanites use city services, particularly if they work in cities. The distinction we want to emphasize is the inability to provide city services to suburban residential areas, not to suburbanites who may commute to cities and obtain services there.

84577

ments, for example, water and air pollution, inadequate water supply, and uncoordinated areawide planning and zoning. Counties more often than cities have the territorial scope to encompass urban problems. Thus, problem resolution and requests for services that cannot be addressed by cities, due to insufficient territorial scope and authority, logically fall to counties.

In 1971, the Office of Management and Budget listed a total of 247 SMSAs in the United States.[18] Of this number, 112 are single-county SMSAs; Florida has six of these and Georgia two. Most of the urban population in both Florida and Georgia, however, resides in multi-county SMSAs. The greater territorial scope of counties, compared with cities, has had a significant impact when examined in light of increased population concentration in metropolitan areas (particularly in the suburbs). The decreasing proportion of central-city populations in SMSAs has produced greater demands in multi-county as well as single-county SMSAs for increased services traditionally provided by municipal units.[19]

Counties have the potential for problem resolution in that they have both the geographical scope and the authority over urban population not residing in cities. The existence of this potential based on territorial scope is a requisite for transforming counties into corporate units. Whether counties will, in fact, function to resolve public problems in a corporate capacity as do cities has not yet been tested empirically. The prerequisite territorial scope, although important, is not sufficient for achieving problem resolution. There are many political, social, and economic conditions independent of territorial scope that affect county resolution of problems generated in urban areas.

Counties predate urbanization, having been in existence long before the rapid urbanization of the past four decades. Given a basic characteristic—population growth—which includes an urban-suburban process, counties are often territorially capable of functioning as "real cities."[20] (A "real city" is a local government which has sufficient territorial scope to encompass an entire urban area including cities, suburbs, and urbanizing rural areas.)

18. See chap. 1n9 for definition of SMSA. When two or more cities of 50,000 inhabitants are within 20 miles of each other, they are included in the same area unless the cities are not economically and socially integrated.

19. Advisory Commission on Intergovernmental Relations, *Profile of County Government* (Washington: U.S. Government Printing Office, 1972), p. 42.

20. George Romney, "The Real City" (Speech delivered to the U.S. Conference of Mayors, Philadelphia, June 1971).

There are exceptions where, due to insufficient territorial scope, counties cannot function as real cities. However, as counties assume an increasingly corporate character and where they have adequate territorial scope, they will be forced to respond to the policy requests of local populations as if they were real cities. Several counties in Florida and Georgia lack sufficient territorial scope to function as such: the Gold Coast of southeastern Florida, from Miami north through Palm Beach, includes three counties; the Tampa–St. Petersburg metropolitan area includes Hillsborough and Pinellas counties; metropolitan Atlanta encompasses seven counties. In these heavily urbanized areas, no single local government encompasses the entire urban population. Yet, the argument can be posited that, even in multi-county areas, it would take far fewer counties to meet the service needs of residents than the sum total of all general local governments. To the extent that fewer governments (counties) lead to a better "fit" over urban populations and result in responsive service delivery, counties approximate the concept of real cities.

CHARACTERISTICS OF COUNTY ORGANIZATION

The average number of counties in the United States is 63 per state; the actual number ranges from 0 in Connecticut, Rhode Island, and Alaska to 254 in Texas. As noted, Florida has 67 counties and Georgia 159.

The Florida total is near the national average, and Florida's counties are larger than Georgia's in both population and territory. Approximately two-thirds of Georgia's counties have populations of less than 25,000, giving Georgia the lowest average population per county in the nation. In addition, Georgia's counties are territorially small. (By contrast, counties in Arizona and California are often geographically as large as Connecticut and Rhode Island combined.)

The population variation of counties in Florida and Georgia ranges from a low of 1,924 in Echols County, Georgia, to a high of 1,311,847 in Dade County, Florida. The median county population in Florida is 108,000 (with 13 counties over 100,000) and 30,000 in Georgia (with 7 counties over 100,000). The wide range of county population size in the two states is obvious. While many of the counties are quite rural, having populations of less than 25,000, there are 20 counties in the two states which are quite urban, with populations of over 100,000.

This wide range in county population size implies that, independent of how counties are organized, the demands upon them will differ. Thus, counties with similar organizational structures may function quite differently, depending upon the size of their populations. Most county organizations are relatively small and govern in accordance with the needs of rural populations; the issues of most concern to the small counties are most likely to be road construction and maintenance, drainage of agricultural lands, and soil conservation measures. Generally, the smaller the county, the fewer services it will provide and the greater the likelihood that the commissioners' concerns will revolve around keeping taxes low.

The large urban counties are confronted with service requests coming from a wide variety of populations. The residents are more likely to want city-type services along with those that the county provides administratively for the state. If the assumption is correct that service requests are in part dependent upon the extent of urbanization, then the urban counties of Florida and Georgia will have a different and more comprehensive set of service demands than the non-urban counties.

COUNTY STRUCTURES

The commission form of county government is used in counties in both Florida and Georgia. This form of county government is, in fact, the most widely used in the United States. Despite the rapid growth of the county-administrator and elected-executive forms of government, slightly more than 2,700 of the nation's 3,106 counties continue to employ the commission form of government.[21] In this governmental structure, county commissioners perform both legislative and administrative activities.[22] There is no separation of powers between the legislative and executive branches, as the county commission has the authority to adopt local ordinances (a legislative function) and to administer services (an administrative function), but there is no single recognized administrator.

As shown in Table 2, the size of county commissions varies across

21. Thomas P. Bruderler, "The Commissioner Form: Assets and Liabilities," *New County Times*, May 13, 1974, p. 7.

22. See William H. Cape, *The Emerging Patterns of County Executives*, Governmental Research Series, no. 35 (University of Kansas, 1967), for a discussion of the functions of county governing bodies.

the United States, with three- and five-member commissions the most common. Governance by committee is the basic style associated with the commission form of government. The commissioners may form committees to oversee the administration of functions in service areas (e.g., a road committee, a welfare committee). The commission members usually have powers to define what problems the county will confront, adopt a county budget, pass ordinances, and administer county functions. Either the commission may carry out all these ac-

TABLE 2
COUNTY ORGANIZATIONAL CHARACTERISTICS: NUMBER AND
SIZE OF BOARD OF COMMISSIONERS

Number of Members of Board of Commissioners	Florida Counties	Georgia Counties	United States Counties
1		26	35
2			15
3		61	1,330
4		1	52
5	64	63	914
6–9	2	7	220
10–14		1	92
15–19	1		79
20–24			76
25–29			61
30 or more			175
Total	67	159	3,049

NOTE: See also Figs. 3, 4.

tivities as a committee of the whole, or the separate members may be responsible for administrative supervision of a particular county function.

The variation in commission size affects how a commission functions. Although the commissioners combine legislative and administrative functions, the larger the commission, the more the functions of government can be subdivided among its members. A single commissioner may take interest and responsibility for a particular activity, such as roads or welfare. A degree of specialization can thus occur among the commissioners in the overseeing of administrative tasks. Such specialization is not possible in counties with single-member commissions, where authority for governing the county rests with one person. Georgia, for example, has 26 counties with single-member

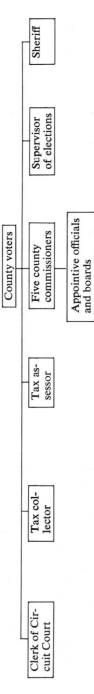

Fig. 3. Commission organization of Florida county government

Note: This chart represents the general organizational pattern. There are exceptions to this model, such as Dade County.

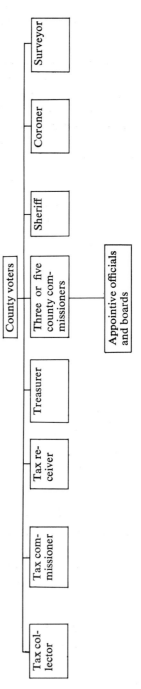

Fig. 4. Commission organization of Georgia county government

Note: This chart represents the general organizational structure. There are exceptions, such as Muscogee County and the twenty-six counties which have one-member commissions.

commissions, out of a total of 35 in the entire United States. Although the commissioner is assisted by various boards and assistants and independently elected county officials, he alone is the "official" county policy-making body.

Figures 3 and 4 depict the typical commission structure of Florida and Georgia counties, illustrating the existence of a plural executive arrangement. These figures show, along with the commission, the independently elected county administrators. These independent executives share policy and administrative responsibility with the commissioners. With the commission formulating policy and administering county government as a whole, the independently elected executives carry out the policies in their functional areas. Since these administrators are independently elected, it is not uncommon for policy differences to exist between them and the commissioners. Typically, independently elected county administrators in Florida and Georgia have these duties:

Sheriff: maintains jail; furnishes police protection in unincorporated areas; carries out orders of the county court.

Treasurer: collects, disburses, and maintains county funds; makes county fiscal reports.

Supervisor of elections: implements candidate and referendum requirements; certifies election returns.

Clerk of circuit court: court administrator; registers and records legal documents.

County surveyor: measures all partitions of lands; surveys all county and district lines; makes all surveys which commission requests.

Coroner: conducts medical investigations to determine cause of death; maintains county morgue.

Tax commissioner: at one time, each county in Georgia had both a tax receiver and a tax collector, but since their duties are related and the peak load of work of these officials comes at different times of the year, the constitution provides that the offices may be combined into the office of tax commissioner.

Tax assessor (or tax commissioner): determines value of all taxable property in the county.

Tax receiver: certifies and totals all county property taxes into a tax digest which goes to county commissioners for determining the tax rate necessary to produce the amount of money needed for the next year.

Tax collector: bills and collects all taxes levied in county.

Although authority within counties is divided among various elected officials, the commission does have a measure of budgetary influence over the independently elected administrators. The commission establishes and adopts the county budget in areas where administration is in the hands of independently elected officials. For example, although the sheriff is the top policy member and administrator of county law enforcement, the commission has the authority to accept or reject the sheriff's budget requests. The sheriff must justify his budgetary requests to the commission. This budgetary linkage between the commission and all independently elected administrators provides an integrating and unifying mechanism for county policy. The commissioners have budgetary power to coordinate and set fiscal priorities on all county programs. However, this budgetary control is not an all-inclusive policy mechanism insuring an integrated county policy, since the administrators have the authority to make all budgetary decisions in their respective functional areas. They determine personnel matters and organizational procedures and objectives. "Politics" is often commonplace, as evidenced by bargaining and conflict between the commission and independently elected administrators with regard to the policy directions pursued.

Two examples will illustrate how policy differences between commissioners and independently elected sheriffs affect problem resolution. The Clarke County, Georgia, Commission was dissatisfied with the management of the sheriff's department. Members of the commission felt that the sheriff was not professional in hiring deputies or in carrying out patrols and investigations. But county commissioners in Georgia are prohibited by the state constitution from removing the sheriff from office; moreover, the constitution provides that the sheriff be provided "adequate" funds for carrying out his responsibilities. Given these restrictions, the Clarke County Commission created a county police department separate from the sheriff's department and made this new department directly responsible to the commission. The Clarke County Police Department has received more revenue appropriations than the Clarke County Sheriff's Department. Clarke County now supports two parallel law enforcement agencies.

Another illustration of how commissioners resolve policy differences is illustrated by budgetary disagreements between the Palm Beach, Florida, County Commission and the independently elected sheriff of Palm Beach County. Florida's constitution, like Georgia's, provides that the sheriff's department be "adequately" funded. Furthermore, Florida has established an appeals process for the sheriff. If he believes he is not adequately funded by the commission, he may appeal the commission's appropriations decisions to the governor and cabinet sitting as the appeals board. In 1974 and 1975, the Palm Beach County Commission cut the sheriff's budget requests. Both years the sheriff appealed the commission's decision to the governor and the cabinet, who ruled in favor of the sheriff, compelling the commission to appropriate the funds requested by him. In 1976, the county commission capitulated. Although several commissioners stated that they didn't approve of the sheriff's budget requests and that they were certain that the requests were out of line with the needs of the department, the commissioners appropriated exactly the funds that had been requested because, they indicated, they knew they would lose at the state level. This is a perfect illustration of state influence.

COUNTY MANAGER FORM OF GOVENMENT

The fastest growing form of county government is that of commission-appointed manager.[23] Of Florida's 67 counties, 29 have appointed managers; of Georgia's 159 counties, 29 have them. In both states, the appointment of a professional manager is a relatively recent organizational change, with most appointments having been made since 1960. The emerging role of managers in Florida and Georgia reflects national trends. In 1974, of 325 appointed managers in the United States, 21 per cent occupied positions created since 1970; currently more than 250 positions (exceeding 77 per cent) have been created since 1960.

Figure 5 shows the organization of governments whose manager is appointed by the county commission. The commission-appointed manager form is an outgrowth of the concept that suggests that county government is a full-time business and needs a manager.[24] The county commission, which is elected, formulates policy. That policy is administered by the commission's agent, the appointed manager. Thus, the commission is free to concentrate on policy while the manager handles the administrative tasks. This organizational form closely follows the city-manager plan, created and developed for cities but adapted to counties.

23. Gary Mann, "Appointed Administrators: Legal Basis," *New County Times*, March 4, 1974, p. 1.
    24. Ibid.

Fig. 5. The basic county manager plan in Florida and Georgia

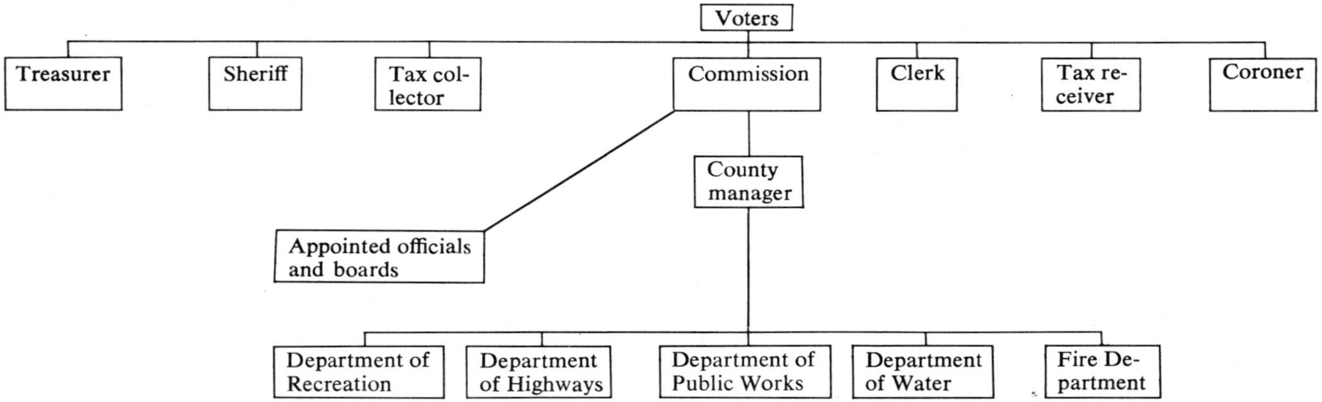

Note: Independently elected administrators may differ in Florida and Georgia.

The organizational form with an appointed manager is designed to achieve three basic objectives. The first is to separate policy making from administration. The proponents of the manager plan argue that policy should be made by an elected legislative body responsible to the citizens. Once policy is formulated, a professional manager should administer it. The second objective is increased professionalism. The appointed manager, a professional, should bring greater economy and efficiency to the functioning of county government. The third objective is to achieve greater policy and administrative coordination, and perhaps the most important impact of the appointed-manager form is greater coordination in the implementation of policy. The manager recommends legislation to the commission and prepares the annual capital budgets for commission approval. Through these various responsibilities, the manager coordinates the county's separate functions, some of which are under the authority of separately elected administrators, into a comprehensive county policy.

A great deal has been written on how managers coordinate local governmental functions and relate to the policy process.[25] The consensus of this literature is that managers may be the most important single policy makers in local government. Most of the literature on managers is based on research conducted in cities, with little study devoted to county managers; however, the consequences of having a manager may be similar in cities and counties whenever the functions and problems of these two forms of local government are the same.

The manager performs a particularly important coordinating role in counties compared to the role he plays in cities. The county commission organizational form makes no distinction between legislative and administrative functions, but the basic organization of cities does make the distinction through the organizationally defined role of mayor. Thus, the county manager brings to the commission form the functional separation between legislative and administrative tasks. The county manager's task is further complicated by the existence of various independently elected officials, whose offices have to be coordinated. The similarities and subtle differences between managing cities and managing counties are in dire need of empirical verification.

The commission–elected-executive form is found in three counties in Florida and Georgia (Dade and Duval counties, Florida, and Mus-

25. Ronald O. Loveridge, *City Managers in Legislative Politics* (Indianapolis: The Bobbs-Merrill Co., Inc., 1971); see his bibliography for an extensive list of research outlining the role of city manager in policy processes.

cogee County, Georgia). This form of county government features executive and legislative branches, established as two separate, counterbalancing, and identifiable parts of the government. The executive is elected at large within the county, making the entire county population his constituency. Therefore, unlike the county manager, the elected executive is not dependent upon the commission for his authority. His authority and responsibilities are specified by the county charter and based upon popular election. The typical responsibilities of an elected executive include preparation of programs for approval by the commission, implementation of the policies approved, responsibility for day-to-day county administration, including budget and personnel control, and submission of the county's operating and capital budgets.[26]

The county elected executive is more than an administrator. He is not only the chief executive but also the top political leader of the county. The elected-executive form combines several advantages. Electing the chief executive ties political leadership to the complex problems of urban counties. Also, an elected executive is likely to be more responsive to the public than an appointed administrator. In addition, vesting the leadership and administration of counties in an elected executive permits the pinpointing of responsibility. The elected county executive's authority and power would approximate those of the separately elected city mayor.

CITY-COUNTY CONSOLIDATION

The organizational forms discussed relate to structures within counties. Counties have also been reorganized territorially through city-county consolidation, which has affected the structural arrangements of cities as well as counties. Urbanization is one of the main stimuli of city-county consolidation. Often demands for services in urban areas cannot be handled within existing municipal boundaries. Portions of urban populations live in both cities and counties, yet the problems and service requests do not neatly cease at jurisdictional boundaries. Thus, city-county consolidation has been the organizational response to attain a better fit between local governments and service needs. A city-county consolidation involves the unification of

26. National Association of Counties, *From America's Counties Today* (Washington: National Association of Counties, 1973).

the governments of one or more cities with the government of the surrounding county.[27] There have been three city-county consolidations in Florida and Georgia. In Florida, these are Miami–Dade County and Jacksonville–Duval County, and in Georgia, Columbus–Muscogee County.[28]

City-county consolidation is the combining of a corporate entity (city) with a territorial entity (county) for the purpose of local service delivery and problem resolution. Organizationally, city-county consolidation is an attempt to create a governmental structure to provide for the urban and suburban populations that "spill over" the existing local governmental boundaries. City-county consolidation is also assumed to achieve other governmental organization objectives: to promote greater efficiency in the provision of services; to reduce the amount of governmental fragmentation, permitting an area to bring together the resources of the central city and surrounding unincorporated county area; and to reduce the need for the creation of special districts or authorities.

In Florida and Georgia, approximately fifteen counties have attempted to adopt city-county consolidation through referenda. Several counties, such as Clarke and Richmond in Georgia, have attempted consolidation more than once. Although the consolidation efforts in these fifteen counties did not receive the necessary voter support, attempts at city-county consolidation will continue in these states, and this organizational form will, in all probability, be adopted in other counties. Many counties in Florida and Georgia feel the necessity for consolidation because they lack the authority to change their servicing and financing arrangements. Consolidation is also considered when counties want to stop governmental fragmentation created by the existence of special districts but lack the authority to set a different kind of taxing arrangement.[29]

In sum, city-county consolidation is an organizational response for adapting county government in order to fulfill the service needs of urban residents. Through consolidation, counties legally obtain corporate status to complement their territorial scope over urban and suburban residents.

27. Rodney L. Kendig, "Trends in County Government," *Municipal Year Book* (Washington: International City Manager Association, 1974), p. 45.
28. Miami–Dade County is officially described as a two-tiered local government. In this work, Miami–Dade County is referred to as a consolidated government in that it possesses most of the characteristics of one.
29. Kendig, "Trends," p. 45.

3

The Frequency and Severity
of County Issues

COUNTY commissioners, in many respects, deal with more diverse agenda of problems than do other local government officials. They must deal not only with problems that arise from the necessity to perform both state-mandated and corporate services but also with problems that arise from both urban and rural settings. In an urbanizing county, for example, commissioners have to perform traditional county functions (road construction and maintenance, tax collection, and collection of vital statistics and records) and also meet demands for increased urban functions (pollution control, industrial development, welfare). These diverse demands complicate commissioners' resolutions of problems. For example, they compound problems of intergovernmental relations. The more urbanized the county, generally the more complex its government. Thus, some problems may affect counties and require commissioners' attention yet may not fall exclusively within county jurisdiction (flood control, water supply, drainage). Or, some problems may arise for commissioners, such as city annexation, simply because there is a diversity of governments within county boundaries. Split demands also compound the problem of finding available resources. In an urbanizing county, there are more diverse demands for scarce resources, and these resources must be shared with other governments. Split demands either cause split loyalties among commissioners or cause commissioners to develop dual perspectives on problems, or both. Either way, the more diverse the agenda of problems, the more difficulty encountered in consensus building among commissioners.

The scope of problems does vary from county to county. While many problems are the same across counties, those in rural counties are different from those in urban counties. What commissioners do will depend largely on the intensity of the problems confronting them. Rural commissioners probably do not have to deal as intensively with people-related problems that arise from needs such as transportation, health care, welfare, and public safety as do commissioners from urban counties. On the other hand, rural commissioners may be more inundated than their urban counterparts by natural resource problems that arise from the need for flood control, irrigation, drainage, and water supply.

By contrast, the agenda of problems for officials of cities and special districts are usually more uniform. While cities must perform a variety of functions, they are not as diverse as those in counties and are usually more limited in scope. Cities are less bound than counties by legal, organizational, and policy directives from the state. The mayor and council members of a city do not have to deal with independently elected officials to the same extent as do county commissioners. Officials from special districts are even more specific in their functions than either city or county officials. Special districts are often local governments concerned with providing a single or limited number of functions. Under the rubric of water management, for example, special purpose water management districts are responsible for providing flood protection, supervising drainage, controlling water uses, and providing recreational facilities. These interrelated functions are limited in scope, compared with the broad array of county functions.

In most studies, the agenda of problems confronting commissioners are dealt with by enumerating the services performed by counties. We contend that an examination of the agenda of problems must go further. Therefore, our analysis in this chapter gives an overview of the problems confronting county commissioners from two perspectives. First, by relying on a survey of 1,026 counties conducted by the ACIR, we give a general assessment of the frequency with which counties deal with problems. We then compare Florida and Georgia county commissioners' attitudes about the severity of twenty selected problems. In both analyses, we examine the differences between urban and non-urban counties.[1]

1. ACIR, *Profile of County Government*, p. 23. The twenty problems selected, as they were classified by issue areas, were regulatory (air pollution,

CLASSIFICATION OF PUBLIC PROBLEMS INTO ISSUE AREAS

In recent years, there have been a number of efforts to classify policy issues, types of policy issues, and policy processes. Lewis A. Froman, Jr., has synthesized many of the major classifications of policy issues used in different media—scholarly literature, mass media, and within government. The most widely used are "traditional" categories of policy: substantive (labor), institutional (congressional), target (farmers), time period (antebellum), ideological (secular), value (good), extent of support (consensus), and governmental level (national, state, local). Less widely used are more abstract classifications of policy which are exemplified by Theodore Lowi's trichotomy of distributive, regulatory, and redistributive; Murray Edelman's dichotomy of material and symbolic; and Froman's designation of city policies as areal or segmental.[2]

Froman notes that "often the most intriguing theoretical work is the most difficult to conceptualize, and vice versa."[3] Principally because there has been little empirical work in drawing adequate theoretical distinctions among public problems, we have concentrated on five issue areas which allow us to classify in a meaningful way the array of public problems which confront county commissioners.

water pollution, preserving open spaces), services and utility (drainage, water supply, solid waste, sewage treatment, flooding), social and remedial (welfare, public health facilities, law enforcement, education, busing), promotion and development (planning and zoning, lack of business and industrial development, housing, roads, recreational development), and governmental and administrative (financing county services, administering county government). When compared to the ACIR's survey of the frequency of function performed by counties, these twenty problems covered the scope of functions mentioned in the ACIR survey. Moreover, these problems encompass those which arise from state-mandated functions, from the impact of federal programs, from the impact of fragmented authorities within the county, and from demands which require counties to perform corporate functions. This array of problems also covers the major expenditure decisions of county commissioners in terms of county programs, funding independently elected officials, and providing matching funds for federal and state programs. See chap. 1n9 for definitions of urban and non-urban.

2. Froman, "The Categorization of Public Content," in *Political Science and Public Policy*, ed. Austin Ranney (Chicago: Markham Publishing Co., 1968), p. 45; Lowi, "American Business, Public Policy, Case-Studies, and Political Theory" (see p. 13n26); Edelman, "Symbols and Political Quiescence," *American Political Science Review* 54 (September 1960): 687–705; Froman, "An Analysis of Public Policies in Cities," *Journal of Politics* 29 (February 1967): 94–108.

3. Froman, "The Categorization of Policy Content," p. 46.

County commissioners must deal directly or indirectly with an array of problems which arise from these necessities: *to regulate certain public and private activities* (e.g., pollution control); *to provide public utility services* (water supply, sewers, solid waste collection and disposal); *to engage in social and remedial programs* (police protection, welfare, and health care); *to promote economic development* (through planning, zoning, and various types of residential, commercial, and industrial development); and *to perform general governmental and administrative functions* (assessment and collection of taxes, administration of elections, operation of lower courts, and recording of legal documents).

Thus, the five issue areas within which we classify public problems confronting county commissioners are regulatory, services and utilities, social and remedial, promotion and development, and governmental and administrative. We discuss these issue areas as to whether they are continuous or non-continuous agenda items for commissioners, whether they involve for commissioners capital, general, or matching program expenditure decisions, whether they affect the community at large or specialized clientele groups, and whether they involve programs initiated by commissioners or by officials in other units and levels of government. These categories, of course, are not mutually exclusive. A problem may fit more than one category. For example, we consider busing in the social and remedial category because it is associated with elementary and secondary education and is a program which is attempting to alleviate educational inequities. But, of course, busing might also be classified as regulatory, since it involves the regulation of policy discretion of local officials.

Regulatory.—Regulatory problems, particularly those associated with urbanized areas, such as pollution control and preserving open spaces, are relatively new activities for county governments. County officials are not usually the initiators of such programs; rather, they react to standards and conditions established by other units of federal or state government. When county officials enforce pollution standards, for example, they are carrying out federal and state regulatory requirements. Grants-in-aid are usually involved to provide an incentive for county officials to enforce federal and state regulatory conditions. In regulating land use by preserving open spaces, many counties, although not all, are reacting to state requirements. Many states in recent years have begun to assert their police power to regulate land uses within the state or to compel local governments to do so through comprehensive planning. Regulatory programs which have been imposed on counties by federal and state programs have required new county organizations (or other local organizations, such as special districts) to carry out the requirements of these programs (e.g., county air pollution control boards). Thus, regulatory activity of this kind constitutes a different agenda item for commissioners.

Commissioners may have authority to appoint boards of directors of these organizations but not to control the policy directives governing the boards' regulatory activities. Hence, there is a potential for conflict between commisssioners and the boards they appoint. There is also potential for conflict between boards and federal and / or state administrators because of pressures on boards to regulate an activity in accordance with constituency and county priorities, on the one hand, and to carry out federal and / or state requirements which may conflict with constituency and county priorities, on the other.

Service and utility.—The service and utility issue area encompasses many problems with which, historically, counties have had to deal because of state abdication, county pre-emption, or prescription by state statutes. State drainage laws are illustrative of a service and utility problem on which the state initially abdicated its authority to the county and subsequently has supported and reinforced county control. The Florida Drainage by Counties Act of 1901 and the Florida General Drainage Act of 1913 were established to allow private landowners to petition county commissioners to establish special purpose drainage districts to drain wetlands. The propensity of the Florida legislature has been not to change this type of local control but rather to encourage and expand it. In 1972, for example, the legislature amended the existing Florida General Drainage Act of 1913 to broaden county authority over the drainage of wetlands.

Also commissioners must cooperate with officials in other units of local governments on service and utility problems. Problems such as drainage, flood control, irrigation, mosquito abatement, and refuse and garbage disposal involve cooperation and coordination with special districts. Other problems, such as ambulance services, fire protection, and sewers and sewage disposal, require large capital expenditures, which counties often cannot finance alone.

The biggest problem in the service and utility issue area is that many of these services need continuous and, in many cases, daily provision of services. While it is possible to close schools during prohibitively inclement weather, to operate the county in the face of a mass transit shutdown, and to forego administrative activities during government holidays, citizens must be provided water, sewage disposal, and fire protection services daily, without interruption.

Social and remedial.—The social and remedial issue area embodies characteristics of the other areas but is also distinguished from them in important ways. Like the service and utility issue areas, many problems in the social and remedial area have traditionally required county programs and services. Unlike service and utility programs which require services to almost the entire populace, social and remedial problems require services to more specialized clientele (e.g., lower income and minority groups and certain disadvantaged groups, many of which require services such as welfare, public health and hospital facilities, and mental health assistance). Also, like service and utility and some promotion and development programs and services, social and remedial programs capture a large proportion of government expenditures. However, unlike most service and utility services and some promotion and development services (e.g., roads), social and remedial programs require fewer capital expenditure decisions for county commissioners. Of course, education building programs require capital expenditures, but these decisions are more often made by school boards than by county commissioners. More than programs in other issue areas, social and remedial programs require redistribution of resources. Social and remedial problems, like problems in other issue areas, are being intensified by urbanization. However, it is more the effects of the stagnant conditions of urbanization (such as population size and density) which affect social and remedial problems than the dynamic conditions of urbanization (such as population change) which affect problems in, for example, the promotion and development issue area.

Promotion and development.—Unlike most problems in the social and remedial and service and utility issue areas, many programs associated with the promotion and development area do not capture the lion's share of government expenditures. However, decisions on promotion and development programs have a significant impact on the socioeconomic character of the community. For example, zoning decisions determine where industrial, commercial, and residential development will take place and the amount of each type of development relative to the others. In effect, many programs associated with promotion and development problems are concerned with stimulating growth (or at least a particular type of growth), whereas programs dealing with problems in other issue areas are concerned with the results of growth. Compare, for example, industrial development and urban renewal with pollution control. Promotion and development programs which do involve capital expenditures cut across several different and very diverse clientele groups. Lower-income groups more than others are affected by public housing and mass transit decisions. But, whereas lower-income groups making demands for certain social and remedial programs stand alone, they are joined on promotion and development issues by key construction industries hoping to build public housing or mass transit facilities.

Governmental and administrative.—Problems in the governmental and administrative issue area are superimposed over all the activities associated with the areas already discussed. Many are associated with routine, everyday activities of running the government, from answering phone calls to keeping records. Other problems associated with the governmental and administrative issue area go to the core of the operations of all programs. For example, raising revenues to finance services involves the basic political question of governance: what amounts will be raised by what method from which citizens, and what amounts will be spent for whose benefit with what results? Thus, governmental and administrative problems in some cases will stimulate little if any clientele interest and in others will stimulate the most intense clientele interest. On routine governmental and administrative problems, no one but county-elected and administrative officials, and perhaps the auditor, will be much concerned. But on questions of revenue and finance, potentially all specialized clientele groups and the general public are vitally affected and therefore concerned.

FREQUENCY OF FUNCTIONS PERFORMED BY COUNTIES

In Table 3, we see the frequency of functions performed by 1,026 counties, both for the five issue areas and for individual functions within areas. The average frequency with which counties engage in social and remedial problems is greater than the average frequency with which they engage in problems in any of the other issue areas. Functions in the governmental and administrative area, as shown in the table, were on average the second most frequently performed, followed by the service and utility area, promotion and development, and regulatory.

Ranking the ten most frequently performed functions (totaling twelve problems because of ties in frequency of functions performed),

Table 3 shows that six are in the social and remedial issue area: jails and detention homes (first), police protection (third), welfare (fifth), public health (tied for seventh with agricultural extension services), medical assistance (eighth), and mental health (tenth). Four of these problems were in the governmental and administrative area: tax assessor and collection (second), coroner's office (fourth), courts (tied for sixth with roads), and prosecutor (ninth). One was in the promotion and development issue area (roads), and one was in the service and utility issue area (agricultural extension services).

Urban and non-urban.—Generally speaking, urban counties more frequently performed functions than did non-urban counties. Although the basic principle applies that large governments perform more functions than small governments, variations existed in the frequency of functions performed by urban and non-urban counties. With the exception of social and remedial problems, urban counties more frequently than non-urban counties were found to perform governmental and administrative, service and utilities, promotion and development, and regulatory functions. As Table 3 shows, this was especially so for governmental and administrative, and regulatory.

For the governmental and administrative issue area, a 17 per cent difference was found between urban and non-urban counties in the frequency of performing functions. This finding suggests that greater responsibilities are placed on urban counties in handling state activities in such functions as administering elections and recording legal documents. In turn, this has required a larger bureaucracy and has increased the need for administrative activities. For example, in the governmental and administrative issue area, very high percentage differences were found between urban and non-urban counties in data processing (36 per cent), central purchasing (26 per cent), and personnel services (19 per cent). Also, it would appear that urban counties must with greater frequency administer programs that arise from crime. Again, the data for individual functions in the governmental and administrative issue area show higher percentage differences between urban and non-urban counties in having a public defender (23 per cent) and a prosecutor (17 per cent).

For regulatory functions, as shown in Table 3, a 10.9 per cent difference was found between urban and non-urban counties. More intense demands are placed on urban county commissioners to regulate private and public activities within their jurisdictional boundaries. In many instances, urban commissioners become involved in func-

TABLE 3
FREQUENCY OF FUNCTIONS PERFORMED BY 1,026 COUNTIES:
URBAN AND NON-URBAN COUNTY DIFFERENCES

	Rank across All Functions	All Counties	(a) Urban	(b) Non-Urban	(a − b) % Difference
Regulatory		18.3	27.6	16.7	10.9
Animal control	23	33	51	30	21
Code enforcement	30	21	42	18	24
Fish and game	36	15	8	16	− 8
Air pollution	37	14	37	10	27
Water pollution	39	12	30	9	21
Power supply	38	13	2	15	−13
Livestock inspection	31	20	23	19	4
Governmental and administrative		48.3	62.6	45.6	17
Tax assessor and collection	2	83	83	83	0
Coroner's office	4	80	87	78	9
Courts	6	76	87	74	13
Prosecutor	9	66	80	63	17
Veterans' affairs	16	49	57	47	10
Personnel services	32	19	35	16	19
Central purchasing	33	18	40	14	26
Data processing	38	13	43	7	36
Public defender	25	31	51	28	23
Social and remedial		54.7	55.7	54.4	1.3
Jails and detention homes	1	85	97	83	14
General assistance– public welfare	5	79	76	79	− 3
Public health	7	75	80	74	6
Medical assistance	8	68	70	67	3
Mental health	10	60	60	58	2
Elementary schools	12	57	37	60	−23
Secondary schools	14	54	36	56	−20
Crippled children	16	49	52	49	3
Special education program	20	40	38	41	− 3
Junior colleges	35	16	27	14	13
4-year colleges	44	3	9	3	6
Hospitals	21	39	41	39	2
Police protection	3	82	78	82	− 4
Probation and parole services	11	59	79	56	23

TABLE 3—*Continued*

	Rank across All Functions	All Counties	(a) Urban	(b) Non-Urban	(a − b) % Difference
Promotion and development		24.5	32.4	23.1	9.2
Roads and highways	6	76	78	76	2
Planning	15	52	76	48	28
Zoning	18	43	55	41	14
Parks and recreation	22	38	55	35	20
Subdivision control	26	30	51	26	25
Industrial development	34	17	21	16	5
Public housing	38	13	19	12	7
Urban renewal	42	5	9	5	4
Mass transit	44	1	5	1	4
Cultural affairs	43	4	7	4	3
Parking	40	9	11	9	2
Museums	38	13	17	12	5
Auditoriums	34	17	17	16	1
Service and utilities		30.3	30.6	30.1	0.5
Agricultural extension services	7	75	75	74	1
Libraries	13	56	57	56	1
Fire protection	17	44	31	46	−15
Ambulance services	22	38	23	40	−17
Airport	24	32	24	34	−10
Solid waste	27	29	37	28	9
Sewers and sewage disposal	28	26	33	24	9
Refuse and garbage	29	23	21	23	−2
Flood and drainage	29	23	34	21	13
Cemeteries	30	21	15	22	−7
Water supply	31	20	21	20	1
Ports and harbors	43	4	9	3	6
Irrigation	41	6	3	7	−4
Soil conservation	19	41	39	41	−3
Mosquito abatement	35	16	37	13	24

SOURCE: Data for this table were derived from ACIR, *Profile of County Government.*

tions previously regulated by cities as problems associated with these functions cut across city boundaries and as they are intensified by urban growth (e.g., increased population size and density). As the state and national governments have become more involved in regulating certain functions, urban counties have become increasingly

more involved in them (i.e., county regulatory activities arise in response to state and national laws). This would seem to explain the
large percentage differences shown in Table 3 between urban and
non-urban counties in the frequency of involvement in regulation of
air pollution (27 per cent) and water pollution (21 per cent).

Several other interesting differences were found between urban and
non-urban counties. First, under the social and remedial category,
non-urban counties were found to be involved more frequently in
elementary and secondary education (−23 and −20 per cent difference, respectively). This is an indication that in urban counties, elementary and secondary education is handled by school districts independent of commissioners' control. In both Florida and Georgia,
school districts are organized on a county-wide basis, with the exception of the largest cities which have independent school districts. Only
in the more urbanized areas are cities large enough (50,000 or
more) to operate comprehensive college preparatory school programs
thought to be necessary by professional associations of school personnel. But in higher education, urban counties were found to be more
involved than non-urban counties (junior college, 13 per cent difference, and 4-year colleges, 6 per cent). Demands for education beyond
elementary and secondary schools are more intense in urban counties,
especially for junior colleges which provide vocational and technical
training.

Second, while promotion and development occur in both urban
and non-urban counties with similar frequency, a greater frequency
of planning (28 per cent difference), subdivision control (25 per
cent), parks and recreation (20 per cent), and zoning (14 per cent)
were found to occur in urban counties. This would seem to be explained by increased demands stimulated by urbanization.

Third, the frequency of service and utilities functions, like social
and remedial, was not found generally to be influenced by urbanization. There was overall only a 0.5 per cent difference between urban
and non-urban counties. These data do indicate, however, that where
functions have not gravitated to cities, then counties provide them.
For example, non-urban counties were found more frequently to
perform functions of fire protection (−15 per cent difference), ambulance services (−17 per cent), refuse and garbage (−2 per cent),
and cemeteries (−7 per cent). In urban counties where there is more
governmental complexity, cities perform these functions. Cities may
also provide these functions on a contract basis for the counties; that

is, a city might provide ambulance service which the county might buy from the city for an agreed-upon price, or vice versa. However, non-urban counties have less governmental complexity and therefore must perform these functions where cities are either unavailable or unable to do so.

Ranking of functions performed: urban and non-urban.—We agree with Thomas R. Dye's assessment that "Often rural counties resemble urban counties about as much as the old-fashioned country store resembles a modern supermarket."[4] However, just as we must exercise caution comparing the country store with the supermarket, we must do so in comparing the functions performed by urban and non-urban counties. We must in both cases determine not just how much is provided but the ordering of what is provided. A supermarket may carry twenty brands of cereal compared to only two brands in the country store, but in both, cereal may be a somewhat less frequently merchandized item than bread or vegetables or meat. The important question, whether comparing supermarkets with country stores or urban with non-urban counties, is whether the items are merchandized differently, not in the quantity of items but in the priority with which the items are ordered. The basics are found in both; is the ordering of the basics within each comparatively different or the same? Do these orderings vary by categories, produce compared to canned goods compared to the meat market? The same kind of questions must be asked when comparing urban and non-urban counties. We know that the frequency of functions performed is different, but what about the ordering within urban counties compared with non-urban counties? Does the ordering vary across issue areas? That is, when urban counties frequently perform governmental and administrative functions, do non-urban counties also frequently perform the same functions in terms of relative frequency?

Although there are large differences between urban and non-urban counties in the intensity of functions performed, Table 4 shows that there is a relatively similar ordering of the frequency of functions performed within each of the five issue areas in both types of counties. When the provision of jails and detention homes, for example, is performed in urban counties more frequently, relative to the provision of four-year colleges, the same general ordering is found in non-urban counties. While this observation holds true generally for the five issue areas, differences were found which have provoking impli-

4. Dye, *Politics in States and Communities,* p. 231.

TABLE 4
SPEARMAN'S RANK ORDER CORRELATIONS FOR THE FREQUENCY
OF FUNCTIONS PERFORMED WITHIN URBAN AND
NON-URBAN COUNTIES

	Urban	Non-Urban	Spearman Rho
Regulatory			.518
Animal control	1	1	
Code enforcement	2	3	
Air pollution	3	6	
Water pollution	4	7	
Livestock inspection	5	2	
Fish and game	6	4	
Power supply	7	5	
Governmental and administrative			.879
Coroner's office	1	2	
Courts	2	3	
Tax assessor and collection	3	1	
Prosecutor	4	4	
Veterans' affairs	5	5	
Public defender	6	6	
Data processing	7	9	
Central purchasing	8	8	
Personnel service	9	7	
Social and remedial			.792
Jails and detention	1	1	
Public health	2	4	
Probation and parole	3	8	
Police protection	4	2	
General assistance– welfare	5	3	
Medical assistance	6	5	
Mental health	7	7	
Crippled children	8	10	
Hospitals	9	12	
Special ed. program	10	11	
Elementary schools	11	6	
Secondary schools	12	9	
Junior colleges	13	13	
4-year colleges	14	14	
Promotion and development			.981
Roads	1	1	
Planning	2	2	
Zoning	3	3	
Parks and recreation	4	4	
Subdivision control	5	5	
Industrial development	6	6	
Public housing	7	8	
Museums	8	9	

TABLE 4—*Continued*

	Urban	Non-Urban	Spearman Rho
Auditoriums	9	7	
Parking	10	10	
Urban renewal	11	11	
Cultural affairs	12	12	
Mass transit	13	13	
Service and utilities			.675
Agricultural extension	1	1	
Libraries	2	2	
Soil conservation	3	4	
Mosquito abatement	4	13	
Solid waste	5	7	
Flood and drainage	6	11	
Sewers and sewage disposal	7	8	
Fire protection	8	3	
Airport	9	6	
Ambulance services	10	5	
Water supply	11	12	
Refuse and garbage	12	9	
Cemeteries	13	10	
Ports and harbors	14	15	
Irrigation	15	14	

cations for assessing the priority of functions performed in urban and non-urban counties. The ordering of the frequency of promotion and development functions performed in urban counties compared to non-urban counties was found to differ only slightly from governmental and administrative functions but was found to differ considerably from regulatory functions. The priorities of promotion and development functions, governmental and administrative functions, and, to a lesser extent, social and remedial functions are similar in both urban and non-urban counties. This was not found to such an extent for service and utility functions and for regulatory functions. Thus, the services merchandized in both urban and non-urban counties, while varying in intensity, have similarly ordered priorities. But this varies by issue areas. This ordering indicates that urban and non-urban counties operate in a more similar way than would be apparent on the surface (albeit with varying intensity); that counties are the most diversified general-purpose local governments; and that both urban and non-urban counties are responsive to similar demands (as indicated especially by their promotion and development and their social and remedial functions). However, in regard to other problems in other issue areas (such as regulatory), urban commissioners differ from their non-urban counterparts and market a different ordering of the products.

ISSUE AREA SEVERITY

In this section, we examine another dimension of county issues. Here, in contrast to the frequency with which county governments perform functions in various areas, we examine how a county commissioner's policy response to a public problem is influenced in large measure by his view of the severity of that problem relative to others. Our assumption is that a commissioner's attitude about the severity of a problem is an indication not only of his concerns about the problem itself but also of his political concerns. Of course, it is theoretically tenuous to draw hard conclusions a priori about the public policy significance of the perceived severity of a problem: problem severity alone does not tell us much about the policy predispositions of a county commissioner. A commissioner may acquiesce in the face of more severe problems; he may pursue solutions more vigorously; he may depend more heavily on other levels of government to assume the responsibility for responding to more severe problems (a subject to be developed in chapter 4). An assessment of problem severity, nonetheless, does provide a basis for comparing the frequency of functions performed with commissioners' attitudes about the severity of issues and for comparing the frequency of functions performed in urban and non-urban counties with urban and non-urban commissioners' attitudes about the severity of issues. Furthermore, it provides a platform for making observations about how county commissioners respond to public problems. For example, if differences are found between the frequency of functions performed and commissioners' attitudes about problem severity (i.e., if counties frequently perform a particular function although the commissioners see it as less severe), we might infer that commissioners are confronted with a conflict between what they feel they should be doing and what they are doing or can do. Constraints (legal, jurisdictional) may be prohibitive. On the other hand, if counties frequently perform a function and commissioners see it as more severe than other problems, then commissioners' attitudes about what they *should* be doing coincide with their behavior as defined by what they *are* doing.

To ascertain commissioners' attitudes about the severity of problems, we categorized twenty selected problems into the same issue areas used to determine the frequency of performance: regulatory, service and utility, social and remedial, promotion and development, and governmental and administrative. Florida and Georgia county commissioners were asked, "Here is a list of problems that your county may now face. Would you please indicate to what degree these are now problems for your county?"

The data in Table 5 show that, among all county commissioners interviewed, the promotion and development issue area was judged to be the most severe. The regulatory area was seen as slightly less severe compared with other areas. Regulatory issues have characteristics which set them apart from the other areas. As indicated, regulatory issues are not continuous agenda items on which citizens make demands on commissioners from week to week; demands for action on regulatory issues are generally directed to other governments, for the limits of policies concerning these issues are by and large established not by county commissioners but by other officials (county, state, or federal). Air and water pollution standards and regulations, for example, have been set by national and state decision makers.

Compare the regulatory issue area with the promotion and development, services and utilities, and social and remedial areas. County commissioners face more continuous demands from their constituents for solutions to problems associated with these areas, although on some of the problems within these areas, like problems in the regulatory area, other governmental decision makers establish the policy boundaries within which commissioners must operate. However, since they are continuous agenda items, commissioners must be involved and take action on a recurring basis.

Although we must exercise caution in comparing the frequency with which functions are performed by counties and Florida and Georgia commissioners' attitudes about issue severity, a comparison of the frequency data and the attitude data (approached with caution) suggests that frequency does not translate into perceived severity. As shown in Table 3, promotion and development were found to encompass the least frequently performed functions. But Table 4 shows that Florida and Georgia commissioners perceived promotion and development problems to be more severe than problems in the other issue areas examined. This suggests that perhaps commissioners are more attuned to the problems in the promotion and development area, problems which are more conducive to having economic effects on important segments of the community than are problems in the other areas.

As shown in Table 5, there are some interesting variations among problems within issue areas. In the governmental and administrative area, for example, commissioners judge financing county services to be considerably more severe than administration of county government. Indeed, financing county services was found to be the most severe of all the problems examined. Financing is a highly competitive, volatile problem, both within government (i.e., among various

TABLE 5
FLORIDA AND GEORGIA COMMISSIONERS' PERCEPTIONS OF THE
SEVERITY OF FIVE ISSUE AREAS BY INDIVIDUAL PROBLEMS
(in percentages)

	High Severity		Low Severity		Total	
	%	N	%	N	%	N
Governmental and administrative	64.2	314	35.8	175	100.0	489
Financing county government	83.3	205	16.7	41	100.0	246
Administering county government	44.9	109	55.1	134	100.0	243
Service and utilities	64.2	789	35.8	440	100.0	1,229
Drainage	68.7	167	31.3	76	100.0	243
Water supply	48.0	118	52.0	128	100.0	246
Solid waste	81.8	202	18.2	45	100.0	247
Sewage treatment	76.6	190	23.4	58	100.0	248
Flooding	45.7	112	54.3	133	100.0	245
Regulatory	58.4	430	41.6	306	100.0	736
Air pollution	52.7	128	47.3	115	100.0	243
Preserving open space	50.6	124	49.4	121	100.0	245
Water pollution	71.8	178	28.2	70	100.0	248
Social and remedial	61.2	746	38.8	472	100.0	1,218
Welfare	69.2	164	30.8	73	100.0	237
Public health facilities	61.0	150	39.0	96	100.0	246
Law enforcement	59.9	148	40.1	99	100.0	247
Education	57.4	140	42.6	104	100.0	244
Busing	59.0	144	41.0	100	100.0	244
Promotion and development	72.0	885	28.0	344	100.0	1,229
Planning and zoning	70.5	170	29.5	71	100.0	241
Lack business and industrial development	66.8	165	33.2	82	100.0	247
Housing	69.9	172	30.1	74	100.0	246
Roads	81.8	202	18.2	45	100.0	247
Recreational development	71.0	176	29.0	72	100.0	248

administrative departments) and between government and outside interests. Financing cuts across all issue areas. Thus, we might expect commissioners to be more actively involved in matters of finance as they affect problem solutions generally and as they affect specific problems. Moreover, financing questions are more volatile than other governmental and administrative problems and those in other areas. General administration by comparison, while cutting across all issue areas, is a more routine, less competitive, less visible activity.

Among those problems in the service and utility area, the data show some interesting variations on perceived problem severity. Water supply and flooding were not seen to be nearly as severe as solid waste and sewage treatment. Water supply and flooding are problems that are generally well controlled. With the exception of the central and southern Florida counties, and even there only at intervals, problems of water supply and flooding arise only sporadically in the two states. These problems do not continuously confront county commissioners, necessitating a response. Moreover, demands for taking action on these problems are by and large directed to other units and levels of government (cities, special districts, or federal agencies). Solid waste management and sewage treatment, on the other hand, are different kinds of agenda items for county commissioners. Although they may be handled by other units and levels of government, county commissioners are themselves continuously involved in taking action on these problems and in providing these services to county residents in the unincorporated areas. This is especially true as growth spills over city boundaries, placing more and more pressure on commissioners to respond. Intense, competing pressures emerge. Homeowners, businesses, and industries demand solid waste and sewage treatment services. Developers need the availability of these services in order to build. Environmentalists create opposition in many instances. Coupled with these pressures are the increased costs associated with provision of these services as well as with increasing the quality of these services to meet state and national standards.

The characteristics of sewage treatment and solid waste management appear to be closely aligned with promotion and development problems. Across-the-board promotion and development problems were considered severe by county commissioners. This was especially true of roads, traditionally a county responsibility.

With the exception of water pollution, problems in the regulatory issue area were seen as relatively less severe than problems in the

other areas. Air pollution and preserving open spaces are new problems on the agenda of county commissioners. The intensity of these problems is confined to specific areas of a county, generally more severe in highly populated areas (which usually means incorporated areas). Therefore, cities are more likely to assume the burden of taking action on these problems. As a result, we might expect commissioners to be less concerned with these problems or to expect these problems to be handled by other units and levels of government.
   Urban and non-urban counties.—How do urban commissioners

TABLE 6
FLORIDA AND GEORGIA URBAN AND NON-URBAN COMMISSIONERS'
PERCEPTIONS OF ISSUE SEVERITY BY INDIVIDUAL PROBLEMS

	Urban		Non-Urban		% Difference
Regulatory	60.2[a]		52.8		7.4
Air pollution		65.0		48.6	16.4
Preserving open space		71.7		43.8	27.9
Water pollution		43.8		66.0	24.0
Service and utilities	77.3		60.0		17.3
Drainage		88.3		62.3	21.0
Water supply		56.7		45.2	11.5
Solid waste		81.7		81.8	− 0.1
Sewage treatment		95.0		70.7	24.3
Flooding		64.4		39.8	24.6
Social and remedial	64.8		60.2		4.6
Welfare		72.9		68.0	4.9
Public health facilities		60.0		61.3	− 1.3
Law enforcement		66.7		57.8	8.9
Education		54.2		58.4	− 4.2
Busing		70.0		55.4	14.6
Promotion and development	64.4		75.0		−10.6
Planning and zoning		64.4		72.5	− 8.1
Lack business and					
industrial development		54.2		73.4	−19.2
Housing		63.3		72.0	− 8.7
Roads		83.3		81.3	2.0
Recreational development		56.7		75.5	−18.8
Governmental and					
administrative	64.4		64.2		0.2
Financing county services		84.5		83.0	1.5
Administering county					
government		45.0		44.8	0.2

a. These figures are the averages of each category.

compare with non-urban commissioners in their perceptions of the severity of problems? The data in Table 6 compare urban and non-urban commissioners' perceptions of severity for the five issue areas as well as for individual problems within each area. The greatest differences between urban and non-urban commissioners were found on regulatory, service and utilities, and promotion and development issues. Urban commissioners were found to consider regulatory (7.4 per cent difference) and service and utility (17.3 per cent) more severe issue areas; non-urban commissioners were found to consider the promotion and development area more severe (-10.6 per cent difference). For the social and remedial and governmental and administrative areas, no large differences were found between urban and non-urban commissioners.

Why do urban commissioners hold that the regulatory and service and utilities issue areas are more severe than do their non-urban counterparts? It would appear that the pressures of expanding growth in urban counties intensify problems in these areas, particularly because they are not handled routinely or completely by other units or levels of government (e.g., cities are not generally involved on a continuous basis with pollution control and preserving open space). Compare this characteristic of regulatory problems with social and remedial problems, an area in which other units and levels of government are involved on a continuous basis. Even small municipalities are expected to assume the main burden of law enforcement for citizens in incorporated areas. Education is largely handled by school districts, mostly independent from county commissioners. States assist counties in welfare administration. Overall, therefore, it would seem that commissioners in urban counties are feeling the burden of regulatory and service and utility problems in unincorporated areas largely because other governments (cities, special districts, state, federal) are not absorbing this burden as much as they are problems in other areas (e.g., social and remedial).

Why do non-urban commissioners hold that promotion and development problems are more severe than do their counterparts in urban counties? Although for different reasons, it appears that the burden of promotion and development problems more often confronts non-urban commissioners because other governments do not relieve them of the necessity of dealing with these problems. Cities handle these problems within their jurisdictional boundaries; the burden outside cities falls to county commissioners. Also, when cities are not available, or, in more rural counties, cities are not able, to handle problems such as lack of business and industrial development, recreation development, housing, and planning and zoning, the county is the unit of government that must respond. In urban counties, these problems are shared with cities, and urban counties have established the tools to deal with them (e.g., planning departments). In non-urban counties the burden for responding to these problems falls almost entirely on county commissioners; they cannot share responsibility for these problems, nor do they have the tools to deal with them.

By comparing the frequency with which counties perform functions (Table 3) with commissioners' perceptions of problem severity (Tables 5 and 6), we gain insight into how the agenda of problems confront county commissioners and require their policy responses. In financing county services, there were virtually no differences found between frequency and severity (tax assessor and collection, 0.0 per cent difference; financing county services, 1.5 per cent). Questions of finance must be dealt with as often in non-urban as in urban counties, and they are perceived to be equally severe by both non-urban and urban commissioners.

In the general administration of county government, there was a large difference between urban and non-urban counties in frequency (collective difference in frequency was 17.0 per cent), but hardly any difference in severity (0.2 per cent). While urban counties are confronted with more administrative problems, they also have more administrative personnel and resources. As far as the severity of general administration is concerned, it seems to confront urban and non-urban commissioners equally. Moreover, the general impression is that non-urban commissioners must intermingle legislative and administrative roles more than urban commissioners, who have larger professional staffs to relieve them of administrative tasks.

Interesting urban and non-urban differences between frequency and severity were also found for planning and zoning. The data in Table 3 show that urban counties more frequently than non-urban counties engage in planning and zoning functions (planning, 28 per cent difference, zoning, 14 per cent); however, the reverse is true for perceptions of the severity of planning and zoning problems (− 8.1 per cent). Non-urban commissioners must deal more often with basic planning and zoning questions than must their urban counterparts. For example, non-urban commissioners more often than urban commissioners must ask in what part of the county they should allow industrial development, commercial development, or residential development. On the other hand, urban commissioners more often than non-urban commissioners must ask what type of zoning variance they should approve.

CONCLUSION

County officials confront a diverse agenda of issues, and the more diverse the agenda, the more difficulty encountered in resolving the issues. Indeed county officials face a wider variety of issues than other local officials from municipalities and special purpose districts. This chapter contains a profile of the diversity of issues confronting county officials, in terms of frequency and severity.

The most frequently performed functions in both urban and non-urban counties were in the social and remedial issue area. As indicated, functions in this area are directed to more specialized clientele, generally require fewer capital expenditure decisions, and involve redistribution of resources. Despite the fact that they are the most frequently performed, functions in the social and remedial area were not perceived by Florida and Georgia county commissioners to be the most severe, but rather the promotion and development area was so seen.

Moreover, the ranking of functions within urban and non-urban counties was found to be more alike for the promotion and development area than for the other areas. In other words, both urban and non-urban counties order promotion and development functions in similar ways. It would appear that both urban and non-urban counties are more involved with and, as indicated by Florida and Georgia commissioners' perceptions of severity, more concerned with an issue area that requires capital expenditure decisions and that most affects major economic interests in the county.

The regulatory issue area was found to be the least frequently performed by both urban and non-urban counties. Less agreement was also found between urban and non-urban counties in the ordering of functions within the regulatory issue area than in the other areas.

Many regulatory functions have only recently been undertaken by counties. These functions (e.g., air and water pollution control and abatement) in many cases are required by state and federal laws, and the counties are compelled to comply with standards established by these laws.

Since counties are a hybrid form of local government performing state-mandated functions, administering federal programs, and responding to the corporate needs of county residents, it is important to examine what county commissioners perceive to be the scope of their responsibilities for various problems.

4

The Scope of Responsibilities

IN the American political system, public problems establish the boundaries of governmental action and become the stimuli to the political process. Ultimately, public problems as they coalesce into policy issues determine the direction governments in the United States take, that is, they determine public policy outputs.[1] As Wayne Francis adroitly points out, "those things about which political scientists ask their questions concerning power, conflict, decision-making, and legal government" are important policy issues.[2]

That public problems shape the direction and scope of policy action taken by government raises some important questions about county governments. How do county commissioners perceive governmental responsibility? Which public problems are viewed as the primary responsibility of the county? Which public problems are viewed as the shared responsibilities of more than one level of government? What configuration of governments do commissioners perceive should be responsible for handling public problems? How does this configuration vary from problem to problem? We will attempt to shed some light on these questions by analyzing Florida and Georgia commissioners' perceptions of needed governmental responsibility on the twenty selected public problems.

Responsibility implies the assumption of a burden. Here it refers to county commissioners' perceptions of needed governmental respon-

1. Jones, *An Introduction to the Study of Public Policy*, pp. 1, 17, 140–44.
2. Francis, *Legislative Issues in the Fifty States* (Chicago: Rand McNally, 1967), pp. 8–9.

sibility, their own and that of other levels of government, on twenty public problems. Governmental responsibility, therefore, indicates which government (county, state, national) and / or configuration of governments (interlocal, local-state, local-national) county commissioners believe should assume the burden of taking action on selected problems.

INTERGOVERNMENTAL RELATIONS IN COUNTIES

County governments occupy a position in the American federal system which necessitates sharing responsibilities with other units and levels of government. Counties administer many state functions and federal programs and are the recipients of federal funds through both grants-in-aid and revenue sharing. Because counties are territorially pervasive throughout almost all the United States, most activities of other local governments (such as cities and special districts) directly or indirectly affect counties.

Counties, therefore, must share governmental responsibility at various levels: interlocal, county-state, and county-national. Interlocal cooperation between counties and other local governments (cities and special districts) in service deliveries occurs through both formally written contracts and informally agreed upon understandings between administrators.[3] Because county-state relationships were established when the republic was organized, the historic role of counties as state administrative subdivisions has been solidified in many functional areas. County-national relationships, either through direct contact or through indirect state administration of federal funds, are also well established. Moreover, in the State and Local Fiscal Assistance Act of 1972, counties were designated as recipients of federal revenue-sharing funds.

The boundaries of many county activities are established by decision makers in other levels of government. An average of approximately 40 per cent of county revenue comes through intergovernmental sources (e.g., state and federal grants).[4] Federal aid, particularly categorical grants, locks counties into specific functional activities. Also, almost all federal grants require matching funds from the county; this means that a portion of county revenue raised from the

3. J. C. Bollens and H. J. Schmandt, *The Metropolis* (New York: Harper and Row, 1965), p. 181.
4. National Association of Counties, *From America's Counties Today*, p. 8.

county's own sources is augmented by other governments. By the same token, a county's operation as a state administrative subdivision means that state statutes mandate many of the county's activities. Counties are not entirely corporate entities like cities, although they must perform corporate functions, and they are not entirely state agencies, although they must administer many state programs as if they were. In effect, then, counties are a hybrid form of local government, which necessitates that they share governmental responsibility with other levels of government.

PERCEIVED GOVERNMENTAL RESPONSIBILITY

A broad assessment of how governmental responsibility is exercised in the American federal system has been provided by the seminal work of Morton Grodzins and refined by Daniel J. Elazar.[5] According to these scholars, sharing is the norm of national, state, and local responsibility for public problems. Grodzins argues, "Functions are not neatly parceled out among the many governments. They are shared functions. It is difficult to find any government activity which does not involve all three of the so-called levels of the federal system."[6]

Table 7 shows that across the twenty selected problems, Florida and Georgia county commissioners perceived that each of the three levels of government in the American federal system should have some responsibility for taking action on these problems but in varying combinations and permutations. The commissioners perceived a wide, divergent range of responsibilities being exercised both by single levels of government (county, state, federal) and by combinations of governments (interlocal, local-state, local-national, and local-state-national). Furthermore, commissioners perceived an almost equal distribution of responsibility between single levels of government (46.6 per cent) and intergovernmental combinations (52.8 per cent). County responsibility was distributed among interlocal (17.0 per cent), local-state (13.0 per cent), and local-state-national (15.5 per cent).

5. Grodzins, *The American Federal System: A New View of Government in the United States*, ed. Daniel J. Elazar (Chicago: Rand McNally, 1966); Elazar, *American Federalism: A View from the States* (New York: Thomas Y. Crowell, 1966).

6. Grodzins, "The Federal System," in American Assembly, *Goals for America* (New York: Prentice-Hall, 1960), p. 226.

When Florida and Georgia commissioners do see other governmental responsibility, it is in the form of a relationship shared with the commissioners, not another unit or level of government operating in isolation. As Table 7 shows, the commissioners are certain that state and federal governments should exercise almost no independent responsibility. Overall, commissioners neither perceived themselves as exercising responsibility in total isolation from other governments nor perceived other levels of government as exercising responsibility

TABLE 7

FLORIDA AND GEORGIA COUNTY COMMISSIONERS' PERCEPTIONS OF
GOVERNMENTAL RESPONSIBILITY ON 20 SELECTED PROBLEMS[a]
(in percentages)

Level of Government	Florida		Georgia		All Respondents
Single level		45.3		47.9	46.6
County	33.2		30.1		31.5
State	7.8		8.4		8.1
Federal	4.3		9.4		7.0
Intergovernmental		54.2		51.6	52.8
Interlocal	18.0		16.2		17.0
Local-state	15.3		11.0		13.0
Local-national	1.1		2.9		2.0
State-national	4.4		6.0		5.3
Local-state-national	15.4		15.5		15.5
Non-governmental		.5		.5	.5
Total		100.00		100.0	99.9

a. In response to the question "Would you please indicate which level of government you feel should take the principal responsibility for handling and solving the following problems?"

without county involvement. This pattern was consistent among Florida and Georgia commissioners. Commissioners in both states expressed general agreement as to the amount and configuration of government that should be responsible for handling and taking action on the twenty problems.

As indicated in Table 7, commissioners perceived the need for a slightly greater amount of interlocal responsibility over the other combinations of intergovernmental responsibility. Similarly, as the states play the role of middleman in the federal system, counties play this role, within states, between the state and other local governments and citizens. For example, counties usually demarcate electoral boundaries for state representatives. On a large number of programs, counties operate as a liaison between cities and the state on services that overlap city and county boundaries (e.g., road construction and maintenance, natural resources, health / hospitals, and welfare).

Interlocal cooperation through interlocal agreements and the transfer or consolidation of functions is also necessitated as counties begin providing municipal or regional services. An ACIR study showed that one of the principal reasons for this occurrence is that "metropolitan county governments still have not markedly diversified their revenue and expenditure responsibilities" and therefore are restricted in expanding services.[7] For example, the study showed that only 16 per cent of county outlays in metropolitan counties are expended for functions that are urban or regional in nature.

Responsibility differences on individual problems.—The American federal system is flexible enough to adapt to changing needs, events, and circumstances. At the conclusion of a voluminous study of intergovernmental relations in the state of Minnesota, William Anderson wrote, "the federal system is a sort of collective name for a mass of different and yet interconnected phenomena."[8] Intergovernmental relations in counties are not exceptions to this characterization; in counties, as well as across the federal system, sharing of governmental responsibilities on public problems shows both differences and interconnections. In other words, the way in which governments in the American federal system respond to public problems allows for variation among problem areas with respect to the exercise of responsibilities. The combinations of governments that take action vary from problem to problem. Elazar says, "The way in which functions are shared varies significantly from program to program." In studying policy issues in all the states, Francis argues that "the behavior of actors and groups of actors . . . will vary significantly from policy area to policy area, and that any general theory will need to account for these differences."[9]

7. ACIR, "The Challenge of Local Governmental Reorganization," vol. 3 of *Substate Regionalism and the Federal System* (Washington: U.S. Government Printing Office, February 1974), pp. 65–68.
8. Anderson, *Intergovernmental Relations in Review* (Minneapolis: University of Minnesota Press, 1969), chap. 9.
9. Elazar, *American Federalism*, pp. 33–34; Francis, *Legislative Issues*, pp. 8–9.

How then do Florida and Georgia county commissioners view governmental responsibility for individual problems? How do their perceptions of governmental responsibilities vary from problem to problem? Figure 6 presents a comparison between those commissioners who perceived that the county should exercise responsibility independently and those who said that there should be intergovernmental responsibility for the selected problems. With the exception of administration of county government, financing county services, and planning and zoning, Florida and Georgia commissioners indicated a need for more intergovernmental responsibility for these problems. Moreover, commissioners indicated that the exercise of governmental responsibility should vary in the amount of both county and intergovernmental responsibilities.

As indicated by Florida and Georgia commissioners, governmental and administration issues are at the core of their authority and responsibility. Through financing of county services and administration of county government, commissioners have a hand in all county activities. For example, almost all those problems for which commissioners indicated that a large share of intergovernmental responsibility should be exercised require county financing through either matching county funds or programmatic funds. They also require county administration.

The problems perceived as requiring the most intergovernmental responsibility have some interesting characteristics. Almost all of them are problems associated with urbanization (water pollution, housing). Many of them involve large capital expenditures (roads, sewage treatment). Some are stimulated by requirements of other governments (air pollution), and some are handled almost exclusively by other governments (education).

Moreover, the problems for which commissioners perceived the greatest amount of intergovernmental responsibility necessary are those more heavily funded by intergovernmental aid. While these problems require county matching funds, they do not consume the bulk of county expenditures. The bulk of county expenditures supports services such as corrections, health and hospitals, and financial administration and general control. Lesser amounts support those problems for which Florida and Georgia commissioners perceived the largest amount of intergovernmental responsibility. It would appear, therefore, that commissioners want to control finances across the board, but on many programs they do not want to raise revenues.

This may be explained in part by the lack of fiscal flexibility commissioners have in raising revenues to fund programs. Commissioners also must react to many programs which are initiated by other governments, such as the state and federal units.

On one hand, the data in Figure 6 indicate the importance of the numerous governments to the county commissioners. Almost across the board, the county commissioners saw themselves exercising responsibility with public officials in other levels of government. This is evident not only on traditionally shared functions such as county-state activities on roads but also on new problems such as air pollution. We suspect this perception of intergovernmental interdependency is stimulated for different reasons. For example, roads have traditionally been a state-county activity, whereas pollution control has been brought about by recent federal legislation. On the other hand, the data in Figure 6 indicate that commissioners perceive the importance of the county government's activities on perceived problems, albeit in varying degrees.

Urban and non-urban commissioners' perceptions of responsibilities.—Increased urbanization[10] in counties contributes to problems of intergovernmental relations. As population growth occurs in counties, problems are intensified, and more governmental units (such as cities and special districts) are created to deal with them. Urban counties resemble federal republics in miniature more so than do non-urban counties. For instance, in urban counties there is a larger mixture of local government (cities and special districts) whose officials have authorities which overlap county authorities. Moreover, in urban counties there is more intense federal and state program involvement. The mixture of governments and the services provided by these governments are a miniature portrait of the larger political system, with many of the same types of socioeconomic and political problems.

Urbanization places a greater burden on counties than on other governments, such as special districts and the state. For example, in examining the transfer of 1,708 municipal functions to other governments, an International City Management Association survey showed that more than a majority of the functional transfers (56 per cent) were to the county, 19 per cent to special districts, 14 per cent to the

10. See chap. 1n9 for definitions of urban and non-urban. Those counties adjoining the central county are also part of the SMSA if certain proportions of their population live and work in the central city.

Fig. 6. County commissioners' perceptions of governmental responsibility by individual problems: county vs. intergovernmental responsibility.

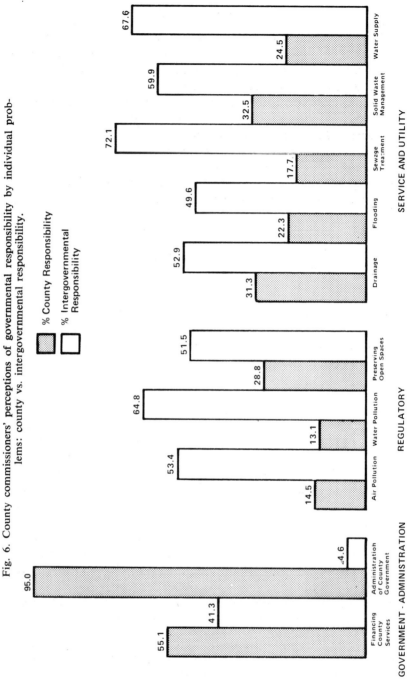

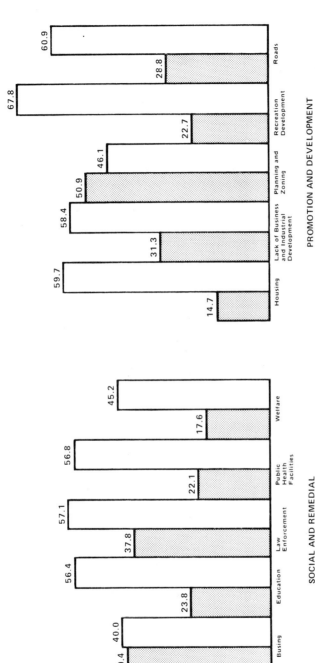

SOCIAL AND REMEDIAL

PROMOTION AND DEVELOPMENT

Note: Comparisons between commissioners' perceptions of intergovernmental and county responsibilities on problems may not total 100 per cent since county is compared to intergovernmental responsibility. All perceptions of single level responsibility for local (except county), state, and federal levels are excluded.

state, 7 per cent to other municipalities, and 4 per cent to councils of government.[11]

Does urbanization increase county commissioners' perceptions of needed governmental responsibility for public problems? As shown in Table 8, on the twenty selected problems, more urban commis-

TABLE 8
COMPARISON OF URBAN AND NON-URBAN COMMISSIONERS'
PERCEPTIONS OF NEEDED GOVERNMENTAL
RESPONSIBILITY ON 20 PROBLEMS

Level	Florida		Georgia		All	
	Urban	Non-Urban	Urban	Non-Urban	Urban	Non-Urban
Single	36.6	49.3	50.7	47.5	40.3	45.9
	(33.6)[a]	(47.0)	(48.4)	(44.7)	(41.0)	(45.9)
Intergovern-	63.4	50.7	49.3	52.5	59.7	54.1
mental (IG)	(66.4)	(53.0)	(51.6)	(55.3)	(59.0)	(54.1)
					100.0	100.0
					(100.0)	(100.0)

a. Percentages in parentheses are for nineteen problems. Administration of county government was eliminated. These percentages show an increase overall since, as we would expect, a large majority of commissioners said that administration should be the sole responsibility of the county.

sioners than non-urban commissioners in Florida and Georgia felt that more intergovernmental responsibility should be exercised. Since governmental complexity is greater in urban counties, we should expect this. The general intensity of finding solutions to problems that arise from increased urbanization seems to necessitate reliance upon other units and levels of government. Urban counties are generally more governmentally complex and confront more intense demands for both human and natural resource services.

While greater intergovernmental responsibility was perceived by urban commissioners overall, the data in Table 8 show a difference in the views of Florida and Georgia commissioners. Urban commissioners in Florida perceived greater intergovernmental responsibility (63.4 per cent) than did urban commissioners in Georgia (49.3 per cent). The difference may reflect the fact that counties in Florida

11. International City Management Association, "Municipal Transfer of Functional Responsibilities," *Urban Data Service Report*, vol. 7, no. 9 (September 1975), p. 9.

are generally larger, and thus more governmentally complex, than counties in Georgia.

The data in Table 9 show the percentage differences between urban and non-urban commissioners' perceptions of intergovernmental responsibility for each of the twenty problems. These data indicate that

TABLE 9
INTERGOVENMENTAL RESPONSIBILITY ON 20 SELECTED
PROBLEMS: DIFFERENCES BETWEEN URBAN AND
NON-URBAN COMMISSIONERS

	(a) Urban	(b) Non-Urban	(a — b) % Difference
Financing county services	42.4	41.0	1.4
Lack of business and industrial development	57.7	60.6	− 2.9
Drainage	73.0	49.1	23.9
Planning and zoning	55.4	43.5	11.9
Welfare	48.2	44.3	3.9
Housing	63.3	60.9	2.4
Roads	69.0	58.4	10.6
Public health facilities	56.0	50.8	5.2
Flood control	57.9	47.1	10.8
Law enforcement	59.6	56.5	3.1
Water supply	68.4	67.3	1.1
Solid waste management	57.9	60.5	− 2.6
Sewage treatment	75.4	70.9	4.5
Air pollution	61.4	50.5	10.9
Recreational development	67.2	68.0	− .8
Administration of county government	5.3	3.3	2.0
Education	60.0	56.2	3.8
Busing	52.2	36.7	15.5
Preserving open spaces	59.6	48.2	11.4
Water pollution	73.7	62.0	11.7

urban commissioners perceived a greater measure of intergovernmental interdependency on all problems than did non-urban commissioners. On only three problems (lack of business and industrial development, solid waste management, and recreational development) did non-urban commissioners indicate that more intergovernmental responsibility should be exercised.

A rank ordering of the twenty problems in Table 9 shows that urban and non-urban commissioners perceived a need for more intergovernmental responsibility on the same problems. Thus, while urban commissioners perceived more intergovernmental responsibility than did non-urban, both order problems almost identically in terms of the relative amount of intergovernmental responsibility that they perceive should be exercised on problems within their counties (r = .989).

The data in Table 10 show that on all but two of the problems (planning and zoning and solid waste management), Florida urban commissioners felt there should be more intergovernmental respon-

TABLE 10
INTERGOVERNMENTAL RESPONSIBILITY ON 20 SELECTED
PROBLEMS: DIFFERENCES BETWEEN FLORIDA AND
GEORGIA URBAN COMMISSIONERS

	(a) Florida	(b) Georgia	(a — b) % Difference
Financing county services	48.7	30.0	18.7
Lack of business and industrial development	59.3	55.6	3.7
Drainage	88.2	60.0	28.2
Planning and zoning	55.2	55.6	— .4
Welfare	52.8	40.0	12.8
Housing	66.6	56.2	10.4
Roads	76.3	55.0	21.3
Public health facilities	64.8	40.0	24.8
Flood control	62.2	50.0	12.2
Law enforcement	64.9	50.0	14.9
Water supply	73.7	57.9	15.8
Solid waste management	56.8	60.0	— 3.2
Sewage treatment	78.9	68.4	10.5
Air pollution	62.2	60.0	2.2
Recreational development	73.7	55.0	18.7
Administration of county government	5.4	5.0	.4
Education	69.4	42.1	27.3
Busing	62.1	35.3	26.8
Preserving open spaces	67.6	45.0	22.6
Water pollution	78.4	65.0	13.4

sibility exercised than did their Georgia counterparts. A rank ordering of the problems, however, shows almost complete agreement between Florida and Georgia urban commissioners on the problems on which most intergovernmental responsibility should be exercised (r = .979).

Problem severity and responsibility.—In discussing the trend toward national decision making, James L. Sundquist argues that problems are initially "seen as local in character, outside the national concern," but later are viewed as beyond the scope of local solution: "as [a problem] persists and as it becomes clear that the states and communities are unable to solve it unaided . . . the activists propose federal aid, but on the basis of helping the states and communities cope with what is still seen as *their* problem." At the end of the sequence, "the locus of basic responsibility" is seen as national.[12] Implicit in Sundquist's argument is the notion that the stimulus to this developmental process of intergovernmental interdependency is problem severity. In responding to public problems, public officials must deal with an array of factors, such as interest group and constituency demands, availability of resources, and the urgency of acting on a problem. "The entire spectrum of these factors impinging on the [public official] constitutes the elements which make up the [official's] perception of the severity of the problem."[13]

We want to determine on which problems more governmental responsibility is perceived to be needed as the problem is perceived to be more severe, and on which problems less governmental responsibility is perceived to be needed as the problem is perceived to be less severe.

The scope of perceived governmental responsibility was obtained by constructing the following continuum, which runs from a perception of non-sharing of responsibility (county) to increasingly more sharing of responsibility (local-state-national). To differentiate between less sharing and more sharing, this continuum was dichotomized by obtaining the grand mean. The commissioners' perceptions of problem severity were examined on a continuum ranging from low to high severity.[14] This continuum was also dichotomized into dimensions (less severe, more severe) by obtaining the grand mean.

LESS SHARING   MORE SHARING

County → Interlocal → Local-State   →   Local-State-National
                          Local-National

The intent was to differentiate among the problems of assessing the direction of perceived responsibility for one problem relative to another according to its perceived severity. Thus, for example, this scheme allows us to classify public problems in terms of severity and

12. Sundquist, *Making Federalism Work* (Washington: The Brookings Institution, 1969), p. 11.
13. Keith E. Hamm, "Intergovernmental Relations as Seen by Florida State Legislators" (Master's thesis, Florida Atlantic University, 1973), pp. 6–7.
14. Issue severity was measured by telling the commissioners "Here is a list of problems that your county may face. Would you please indicate to what degree these are now problems for your county?"

sharing in a preliminary way according to the quadrants shown in Table 11. Problems located in quadrant I, for example, would be characterized by lower severity and less sharing; problems in IV would be characterized by higher severity and more sharing.

TABLE 11
CLASSIFICATION OF 20 SELECTED PROBLEMS BY SEVERITY
AND SHARING

	Less Severe	More Severe
	I	**II**
Less sharing	Administration of county government Water supply Law enforcement Busing	Drainage Lack of business and industrial development Planning and zoning Financing county services Solid waste management
	III	**IV**
More sharing	Flooding Air pollution Preserving open spaces Public health facilities Education	Housing Welfare Recreational development Water pollution Sewage treatment Roads

Table 11 places the twenty problems in the severity-sharing quadrants. This classification is intended only to be suggestive of trends in the sharing of governmental responsibility according to problem severity. Even with this caveat, these data reveal some interesting patterns. In the less severe–less sharing category (quadrant I), we find problems which, by and large, do not require large capital outlays by counties (busing, law enforcement, administration) and problems which are handled by units or levels of government other than county commissioners. For example, law enforcement in the incorporated areas comes under the jurisdiction of the municipal police force and within the unincorporated areas under the jurisdiction of the sheriff, who is generally an independently elected county official.

In the less severe–more sharing category (quadrant III), again we find few problems that require outlays of county revenues (preserving open spaces, air pollution, education). Florida and Georgia, for example, establish a tax rate for school districts; counties are generally fiscal conduits for these districts in terms of approving their budgets. Flood control is also a problem for which commissioners depend on outside technical and fiscal assistance; it is thus not a continuous problem for the commissioners.

Those problems in the more severe–less sharing category (quadrant II) are ones that are not seen as intergovernmental problems even when they are perceived to be severe. Why is the developmental process not operating on these problems? The problems in quadrant II are, by and large, ones over which county commissioners are able to exercise more independent authority, and about which they can make policy decisions without overstepping the boundaries of state or federal laws. On planning and zoning matters, for example, county commissioners possess the authority to respond to requests for zoning changes. This is seen as a more severe problem but one over which county commissioners feel they can exercise control. Compare planning and zoning to problems such as housing, welfare, water pollution, sewage treatment, roads, and even recreational development— those problems found in the more severe–more sharing category (quadrant IV). On each of the problems, the limits of county commissioners' decision making are established, to some degree. On sewage treatment construction, for example, commissioners must adhere to a variety of federal conditions to be able to receive 75 per cent construction funding under the Federal Water Pollution Control Act Amendments of 1972. A similar situation exists for the other problems: either state or federal conditions, or both, establish the limits of commissioners' decisions; therefore, of necessity they must look to other governments to share problem responsibility. Our findings illustrate that Sundquist's developmental thesis operates but only on certain types of problems, those which are mandated to the county by other governments or those which require the county to work within the confines of other governmental officials' decisions.

CONCLUSION

In examining county commissioners' perceptions of intergovernmental responsibility, we found some interesting nuances about how the federal system ought to operate in counties. Although Florida and Georgia county commissioners indicated that intergovernmental responsibility should be exercised on almost all the problems examined, they also indicated that they should retain some measure of independence in exercising responsibility. Moreover, Florida and Georgia commissioners did not feel that officials in other units of local government (cities and special purpose districts) and at other levels of government (state and federal) should exercise independent responsibility without commissioners' involvement.

The amount of intergovernmental responsibility which commissioners perceived was found to vary from problem to problem. The most intense intergovernmental responsibility was found to be associated with urbanization and to involve problems which require large capital expenditures and over which county commissioners cannot exercise independent judgment. Problem severity also caused the commissioners to see a need for more intergovernmental responsibility, particularly on problems which are mandated by other governments (i.e., problems on which commissioners' decisions are formulated within the limits established by officials in other units and levels of government). On the other hand, Florida and Georgia commissioners perceived themselves as exercising more independent responsibility over corporate problems not mandated by other governments, even though these problems were perceived to be severe. Finally, urban county commissioners saw more need for intergovernmental responsibility than did non-urban commissioners, especially in Florida.

These findings suggest a further and more tentative conclusion about intergovernmental responsibility. The differences found between urban commissioners in Florida and Georgia on their perceptions of responsibility suggest that sharing varies not only from urban to non-urban counties but also from state to state. This points to a complex federal system, one which has consequences for how one deals with public problems. For example, our findings suggest that politics initiated by the federal government may receive different implementation by Florida commissioners than by Georgia commissioners.

Jeffrey L. Pressman and Aaron Wildavsky have pointed out the effects of the federal system on implementing federal programs through state and local processes: "No one supposes the federal system is going to disappear. If the federal principle maintains its vitality, then it means precisely that state and local organizations must be able to oppose, delay, and reject federal initiatives. When these kinds of actions can no longer be undertaken, there is no state or local independence and hence no operative federalism."[15] Our analysis not only confirms this generalization (see particularly Table 7) but also suggests that the "opposition," the "delay," and the "rejection" by local organizations will vary from state to state and thus further complicate the implementation of federal programs.

15. Pressman and Wildavsky, *Implementation* (Berkeley: University of California Press, 1973), p. 161.

5

Commissioners' Policy Orientations

HOW commissioners approach their jobs as policy makers affects not only the problems they choose to resolve but also how they go about making decisions on these problems. Although county commissioners have the authority both to make policies and to administer the policies they formulate, it is not known if they do, in fact, approach their jobs as both legislators and administrators. We assume, for instance, that formulating a policy on road construction and maintenance is very different from administering road activities. The administration of road construction programs requires a high level of professional training. Most commissioners are part-time officials, not professional administrators, and the demands of earning a livelihood, as well as their constrained time schedules, inhibit them from fully developing the technical expertise needed to administer such programs.

Additionally, county commissioners must make decisions on a wide range of programs and services. Most such decisions are quite routine, and there may be widespread agreement as to what should be done concerning these routine functions, for example, decisions regarding road construction, since counties have been providing road construction for many years. And so, although road construction may be expensive, it may not be difficult for commissioners to make decisions on roads. On the other hand, zoning decisions may cause difficulty. There may be little agreement among the commissioners as to what decision to make in response to conflicting demands from various groups for zoning changes. Rezoning necessitates changes in existing land-use patterns; often the opponents and proponents of change request vastly different decisions from the commissioners. Land zoning and rezoning are also relatively new problems confronting counties; procedures for making such decisions have not been routinized as they have been in the more traditional service areas such as roads. As recently as 1971, approximately 500 of the nation's 3,000 counties had the authority to zone land, and most of these counties were in urban areas.[1]

In this chapter, we focus on how the commissioners view their policy activities and how they approach decisions on the major problem areas confronting their counties.

POLICY ACTIVITIES: LEGISLATIVE AND ADMINISTRATIVE

The separation-of-powers model is familiar to all students of American government. The basic tenet of this model is, of course, that the legislative, administrative, and judicial functions should be separate. The national government was structured in this way and provides the model for local governmental organization. Concern and debate has focused on how and to what extent these functions should be separated at the local level. A central question arises when this model is applied to local government: if local governmental functions are separate, how does this affect basic political processes and resultant policies?

As in most states, the county governing body (commission) in Florida and Georgia is legally structured to perform both legislative and administrative functions. The judicial branch is separate.[2] But do commissioners engage in both legislative and administrative activities and, if so, to what extent? Our purpose is to determine if commissioners perceive a legislative-administrative dichotomy in the activities they perform and what accounts for the dichotomy. County commissioners can legislate local ordinances and administer the provision of almost all services and functions if they choose to do so. But the extent to which county commissioners actually engage in both legislative and administrative functions has not been systematically assessed. For purposes of analysis, we identify a commissioner's policy-related activities as a mix of both legislative and administrative involvement in the major service areas provided by counties. We approach the question by examining the Florida and Georgia com-

1. ACIR, *Profile of County Government*, p. 10.
2. Wager, *County Government across the Nation*, pp. 9–10.

missioners' perceptions of their legislative and administrative policy activities.

Urbanization and policy activities.—We further theorize that job activity is related to urbanization and governmental structure. Sociologists, particularly Emile Durkheim, have long identified division of labor and specialization of function as hallmarks of urbanization.[3] In explaining the job activities of county commissioners, we hypothesize that urbanization necessitates a separation of functions. As government grows and becomes more complex, administrative and legislative functions can best be performed by separating the activities to achieve higher levels of specialization and expertise. We would expect, therefore, to find a relationship between the urbanization of counties and the provision of an increased number of specialized public services. Urban counties are confronted with complex public problems that require constant monitoring by their elected commissioners. Likewise, in urban areas the administration of government becomes a specialized activity which is more difficult to perform continuously and routinely by commissioners than is the case in less urban areas. Urban counties provide a wide array of highly technical services such as air pollution control, the supplying of water and sewage, planning and zoning functions, and so on. Such services require high levels of expertise which are difficult for part-time commissioners to administer. To administer technical and complex programs requires full-time professional administration.

More than a decade ago, John E. Stoner noted, "Both the volume and nature of the functions performed by boards of county commissioners have necessitated their becoming deliberative bodies. But many county boards, partly by custom and partly as the result of the expectation of their citizens, still operate merely in an administrative capacity."[4] He did not deal with the effects of urbanization on county commissioners' performances. It would seem that county commissioners from urban areas, as distinct from rural areas, would be least able to engage primarily in administrative activities and would function primarily as legislators.[5]

3. Durkheim, *The Division of Labor in Society*, trans. George Simpson (New York: The Free Press, 1960), p. 257.
4. Stoner, *Indiana County Commissioners as Policy-Makers*, Indiana Public Affairs Notes (Bloomington: Bureau of Government Research, May–June 1962), p. 1.
5. For a thorough analysis and discussion of legislative behavior, see John

One means of separating legislative and administrative functions is for a single commissioner to assume administrative control over a functional area, for example, one commissioner would administer roads, another recreational functions, and so on. Although the assignment of commissioners to administer specific functions does not necessitate legal division of legislative and administrative functions, it may in fact achieve a separation of functions between the commission as a whole and the administrative activities of each commissioner.

A more direct way of making the distinction between legislative and administrative activity is by reforming the structure of government to separate the two functions into distinct branches. The basic local government reform model proposes a separation whereby a council (commission) performs the legislative functions and a manager heads the administrative branch. Unlike the federal government where the two branches are constitutionally equal, at the local level the administration is legally dependent upon the governing board. The county board of commissioners appoints the manager (by majority vote), and he serves until he no longer has majority support. The manager is responsible for the administration of the county functions. By definition, having a manager not only necessitates a separation between the legislative and administrative activities but also makes the legislative body dependent upon the executive in administrative matters.[6]

The data in Table 12 categorize commissioners' policy activities into seven spheres. These seven policy activities were divided into the two basic policy areas of legislative and administrative activities. Our intent in subdividing legislative and administrative activities was to capture the basic decisional functions of the county commission and compare them to those of any policy body.[7] In assessing

C. Wahlke, Heinz Eulau, William Buchanan, and Leroy C. Furguson, *The Legislative System* (New York: John Wiley and Sons, 1962).

6. Although this study focuses on county commissioners and administrators who are appointed by the governing body of the county and serve at its pleasure, there is a form of county structure in which the administrator is elected. The elected-administrator type of county government embodies the separation-of-powers principle between the executive and legislative branches. Throughout the nation, most county administrators are appointed (325) rather than elected (50). The appointed-administrator county structure is characteristic of the county governmental structure found in Florida and Georgia. See Mann, "Appointed Administrators: Legal Basis."

7. See Harold D. Lasswell, "The Decision Process," in *Politics and Social*

TABLE 12

COUNTY COMMISSIONERS' PERCEPTIONS OF THEIR POLICY ACTIVITIES IN EIGHT PROBLEM AREAS

(in percentages)

Problem Area	(1) Define problem	(2) Bring problem to attention of commission	(3) Determine if county should engage in activity	(4) Establish what should be done with regard to problem	(5) Scrutinize what is recommended by county administrators	(6) Close supervision of county administrators	(7) Actually take a hand in county administrative matters	Mean percentages
Financing county services (N = 237)	32.0	34.8	40.3	43.5	36.7	39.1	49.8	39.5
Welfare (N = 198)	17.2	21.7	28.1	29.2	32.8	17.0	17.8	23.4
Roads (N = 236)	28.8	40.0	35.2	42.3	37.1	36.7	44.3	37.8
Solid waste management (N = 191)	22.1	24.9	28.1	32.0	29.2	21.7	26.5	26.3
Planning and zoning (N = 200)	22.1	24.5	29.6	32.8	27.3	21.3	26.5	26.3
Water supply (N = 163)	19.0	21.3	24.1	24.9	19.4	14.2	17.8	20.1
Law enforcement (N = 185)	15.8	27.3	20.1	27.7	29.2	18.6	15.0	21.9
Recreational development (N = 209)	22.5	31.2	30.4	33.6	31.2	22.9	28.5	28.6
Mean percentages	22.4	28.2	31.6	33.2	30.2	23.9	28.3	28.0

Policy Activity

county commissions, we have relied upon Lasswell's classification of major generic components of the decision process. Basically, the seven policy components range across the decision process in a temporal sequence from the first stage of recognizing and defining problems to the final stage of actual administration of programs designed to treat defined problems. Although problem resolution may not be complete with program administration, we feel the classification does capture the major components of commissioners' policy activities.

Although the commissioners have the authority to perform all seven of these activities for each of the eight problem areas, Table 12 indicates that they specialize and concentrate more on some activities than on others.[8] In the table, the numbers in the problem area column range from a high of 237 for financing county services to a low of 163 for water supply. (An N of 237 for financing county services means that, of our total sample of 253 commissioners, 237 participated in at least one of the seven policy activities dealing with financing county services.) Commissioners often selected more than one policy activity for each of the eight functions. This is reflected in the percentages listed for each policy activity performed in each problem area and indicates why the percentages do not total 100.

Our major interest in these seven policy activities is to determine whether commissioners are performing basically legislative or administrative activities. Also, we examine the extent to which legislative and administrative activities are related to different policy areas. The first six policy activities are generally considered legislative functions. Of these six legislative activities, the first four deal with the initial stages of the legislative process of defining problems and determining if a commission should take action. Policy activities five and six are basically oversight functions, that is, commissioners monitoring administrators in their approach to problem resolution. The seventh activity is purely administrative.

As shown in the table, commissioners were asked to indicate their legislative and administrative activities in the eight major problem areas of county government (table columns), finance*, roads*, welfare†, law enforcement†, water resources†, solid waste management†, planning and zoning†, and recreational development†.[9] Excluding

Life, ed. Nelson W. Polsby, Robert A. Dentler, and Paul A. Smith (Boston: Houghton Mifflin Company, 1963), pp. 93–105.

8. Ibid., p. 94.

9. *Traditional county functions; †non-traditional county functions. The

education, these eight problem areas consume more than 90 per cent of a county's tax resources and are considered by most students of local government as the major problem areas. Commissioners were asked questions concerning their administrative and legislative involvement in each of these functional areas (see Appendix B).

Table 12 indicates that the commissioners basically view their policy activities as both legislative and administrative in all problem areas. Depending upon the problem area involved, the proportion of commissioners mentioning legislative-administrative activities varies. Commissioners engage in more administrative activities in the traditional areas of county service delivery. In particular, they engage in administrative activities in financing county services (49.8 per cent) and roads (44.3 per cent) to a greater extent than for any of the non-traditional functions. These traditional functions have been delivered by counties as long as counties have been in existence, and commissioners continue to administer these services to a greater extent than the non-traditional services. In fact, in these two traditional areas, in comparison to the six non-traditional problem areas, the commissioners perform more policy activities in both legislative and administrative dimensions.

Although commissioners engage in all six of the defined legislative policy activities, there is variation. Approximately one-third of the commissioners reported that they established what the county should do in a problem area or they brought the problem to the attention of the commission (col. 4). The commissioners engaged to a slightly lesser degree in oversight activities, such as scrutinizing and supervising administrators. A relatively small proportion of the commissioners acted as policy initiators for all of the problem areas. With a mean of 22.4 per cent, approximately one-fifth of the commissioners indicated that they defined problem areas.

Commissioners are legally responsible for administering county

---

distinction between types of service is based upon traditional services, provided by counties upon their creation and mandated by state legislation or constitutional provisions, and non-traditional services, provided subsequent to the creation of counties and tending to be provided by those more densely populated areas of counties within metropolitan areas. The purpose of developing this distinction is to get at the historical roots of service delivery from an administrative-legislative perspective. Our definition of "traditional" and "non-traditional" services is consistent with that used by the ACIR, thus allowing the opportunity to compare our results with the largest collected body of data on county services. See ACIR, *Profile of County Government*, p. 22.

policies. Yet, for each of the eight problem areas examined, less than half of the commissioners indicated administrative activity. For most problem areas, the administrative involvement was performed by much less than one-half of the commissioners. The mean administrative score across all eight problem areas was 28.3 per cent, with financing county services being highest (49.8 per cent) and law enforcement engaging the least administrative involvement from commissioners (15.0 per cent).

The commissioners' administrative activities in law enforcement represent an interesting test of the thesis of separation of functions. Fifteen per cent of the commissioners said they actually took a hand in county administrative matters dealing with law enforcement, a traditional county service administered by a sheriff who is elected independently from county commissioners. It is a service that receives a great deal of attention in most counties. These commissioners perceive it necessary to stay informed concerning what the sheriff is doing. This perception of commissioner involvement is quite interesting in that, from another perspective, it may represent how they wish they could keep some control over the sheriff's department. The office of sheriff, compared to other elected county administrators such as the tax assessor, is very visible to the public. The commissioners may be perceiving that, although the sheriff is an elected official, they themselves are administering on behalf of the public in an area of high visibility and importance.

The commissioners see less separation between the commission and sheriff in the administration of law enforcement than the organizational charts in chapter 2 indicate. The charts imply that the sheriff administers law enforcement. This is accurate, but, from the perspective of some commissioners, they are also administering law enforcement. It could be argued that the reason commissioners engage in this role is that, although there is an independently elected officer, they must be responsive to the public "needs." The commissioners receive more public contact on law enforcement matters than on any other problem area and thus feel that they must actively assist the sheriff in his activities. They may perceive that law enforcement is too important to be administered exclusively by the sheriff.

Several problem areas which are not administered by a separately elected official receive little administrative attention from commissioners. Approximately 18 per cent of the commissioners indicated that they actually took an administrative hand in welfare or water supply matters, very close to the 15 per cent figure for the law enforcement function, which does have a separately elected administrator. Perhaps the visibility and importance of welfare and water supply are not sufficient for commissioners to engage in administration. In large counties both of these functions are administered by professionals. In addition, welfare matters are highly regulated by state and federal statutes and guidelines. The issues in these two areas are highly specialized and technical in nature, particularly in the case of supplying water, where criteria based upon sound engineering standards must be applied. State and federal regulations on welfare benefits are detailed and must be met in all counties. Therefore, there is little for the commissioners to administer in these areas. Of course, commissioners have the authority to supply additional areas with water or to expand welfare benefits beyond state and federal requirements, but their policy activities include very little administrative involvement. The commissioners retain control in these areas through their authority to appoint administrators, but once administrators are appointed, there is little interference from commissioners.

URBANIZATION AND STRUCTURE: A POLICY TEST

Our concept of urbanization was measured by the indicators of county size in 1970, county density in 1970, and population change in 1960–70.[10] Our sample of county governments reflected a broad range of urbanization, from the smallest county with a population of 3,000 to the largest with well over a million, the median county size being 25,000. County governmental structure was measured by the existence of a manager who was responsible to the commission for the administration of functions. All counties having appointed managers were classified as reformed.

The legislative-administrative activities were examined by two additional methods. First, separate administrative and legislative scales were created for the combined eight major functional areas used in Table 13. The scales were based on the commissioners' cumulative involvement in the eight areas.[11] That is, we were interested in the

10. For a discussion of these three indicators of urbanization, see Heinz Eulau and Kenneth Prewitt, *Labyrinths of Democracy: Adaptations, Linkages, Representation and Policies in Urban Politics* (Indianapolis: The Bobbs-Merrill Co., 1973), p. 67.

11. The problem put was "We would like to get some indication of what

commissioners' general legislative and administrative perceptions of activities across all eight functions. The second method of examining job activities was based upon creating a measure for each of the eight areas. These eight indexes allowed us to examine what service areas received the most attention from commissioners.

TABLE 13

URBANIZATION AND GOVERNMENTAL STRUCTURE CORRELATED
WITH COMMISSIONERS' JOB PERCEPTIONS OF
ADMINISTRATIVE AND LEGISLATIVE
ACTIVITIES

	Administrative Activity	Legislative Activity
Urbanization	Simple	Simple
1970 population	−.07	.11
1970 density	−.17	−.05
1960–70 population change	−.14	.06
	Multiple r = .19	Multiple r = .20
Governmental structure	Simple	Simple
Existence of county manager (N = 253)	−.18	.03

Counties were originally created as administrative sub-units of the state, so we felt that the legislative-administrative mix of commissioners' activities would vary across functions, with traditional—i.e., state-mandated—functions requiring more administrative activities and non-traditional functions necessitating legislative activities. This is because non-traditional functions are performed primarily in response to citizen demands rather than to administrative requirements established by the state.[12]

We did not find any significant relationship between urbanization and the perceived job activity of the county commissioners. As shown in Table 13, correlation coefficients of less than ±.20 were found between urbanization and the indexes for job activities performed

---

activities a county commissioner's job entails. Would you indicate if you engage in the following activities . . ." (a) actually take a hand in county administrative matters (administrative scale from 8 functions); (b) establish what would be done with regard to a problem (legislative scale from 8 functions).

12. A total of ten scales were developed, one administrative and one legislative for the combined eight functions and an activity scale for each of the eight functional areas.

TABLE 14
URBANIZATION AND GOVERNMENTAL REFORM CORRELATED WITH COMMISSIONERS' PERCEPTIONS FOR EIGHT SEPARATE JOB ACTIVITIES

Urbanization	Finance	Welfare	Roads	Sewer/Water Management	Planning and Zoning	Water	Law	Recreation
1970 population	.03	.12	.05	.06	.10	.16	.14	.08
1970 density	−.06	−.02	−.10	.00	.00	.07	.01	.01
Population change 1960–70	−.08	.10	−.09	.03	.16	.18	−.05	.03
Governmental structure existence of county managers (N = 253)	−.12	−.08	.07	−.18	−.14	−.25	−.15	.15

(i.e., administrative and legislative). Although the relationship between several indicators of urbanization and administrative activity is in the expected negative direction, the correlation coefficients are very small. The highest correlation coefficient of −.17 (1970 population density) accounts for approximately 3 per cent of the variation in the administrative job activity index. Also, no significant relationship was found between urbanization and the legislative index.

As shown in Table 14, generalization was consistent for each of the eight problem areas. This table shows that urbanization was not highly related to how county commissioners perceived job activities for any of the areas. Our analysis indicates that urbanization and the existence of a county manager do not importantly influence commissioners' policy activities. None of the indicators of urbanization had statistically significant relationships with the job activities, nor were they related to the amount of county commissioners' involvement in any of the eight areas (see Tables 13 and 14). The weight of the analysis indicated little variation between urbanization and job activities. The highest correlation coefficient of $r = .18$ was between population change 1960–70 and involvement with water service. This "high" r of .18 accounts for 3 per cent of the variation. All the remaining correlation coefficients are smaller. Clearly, urbanization was not the explanation for legislative and administrative involvement we were seeking.

We also found that a reformed county structure, like urbanization, had little effect upon the commissioners' perceived job activities. Tables 13 and 14 show the correlation coefficients between the existence of an appointed county manager and the administration and legislative indexes, as well as for the eight functional areas. The correlation coefficients were quite small in all cases. The presence of an appointed county administrator made little difference when the county commissioners were asked whether they saw themselves generally as administrators or as legislators. Nor was the existence of a county administrator significantly related to legislative or administrative activity in any of the eight areas (Table 14).

Urbanization and governmental structure do not explain the general legislative or administrative perception of job activity. Nor do these concepts explain commissions' involvement in the eight functional areas. The data thus suggest that there are several limits to the urbanization and reform arguments for explaining job activities of county commissioners.

HISTORY AND LAW

Our analysis of commissioners' perceptions of job activity necessitates a re-examination of commissioners' roles in county government. We must consider the effects of law and historical precedent upon commissioners' activities and involvement in service areas. Though difficult to measure empirically, some crucial observations can be made regarding their impact on commissioners' job activities.

Two factors provide a context for explaining legislative and administrative involvement. First, state government places legal constraints upon counties and the prescribed functions they perform. Second, historical precedent in the development of county government has placed importance upon certain functions, such as roads and

TABLE 15
COMMISSIONERS CLAIMING ADMINISTRATIVE AND/OR
LEGISLATIVE ACTIVITY IN EIGHT
FUNCTIONAL AREAS
(in percentages)

Function	Commissioners Engaging in Administrative Activity	Commissioners Engaging in Legislative Activity
Traditional		
Finance	49.8	43.5
Roads	44.3	42.3
Non-traditional		
Solid waste management	26.5	32.0
Planning and zoning	26.5	32.8
Recreation development	28.5	33.6
Welfare	17.8	29.2
Water problems	17.8	24.9
Law enforcement[a]	15.0	27.7

N = 253

a. Law enforcement is mandated by the state. However, we have categorized it as non-traditional because counties provide much more in the area of law enforcement than is required by the state. Counties have developed patrol and investigative capacities, whereas the traditional role of the sheriff is only that of officer of the court. Thus, for theoretical purposes, to determine the scope of commissioners' job activities, law enforcement is categorized as non-traditional. If the sheriff acted exclusively as officer of the court, then law enforcement would have been categorized as a traditional service.

finance, which have continuing influence upon present-day activities of county commissioners.

As is common in the South, counties historically have been relied upon as the primary unit of local government for service delivery and as a political base. This is particularly true in Florida and Georgia, which inherited English common law and charters which did not make a legislative-administrative distinction in local government. The early English background and influence are also seen today in many of the designated officials of county government, such as the sheriff.

Traditionally, county services centered principally around the collection of state taxes and road construction and maintenance. For example, the first board of commissioners established in 1869 by the Georgia General Assembly was known as "commissioners of roads and revenue." This designation was not changed until 1964, when the Georgia Assembly changed the name to Board of Commissioners. Viewing the historical title, it may not be surprising that the two functions in which commissioners continue to engage actively are roads and finances (Table 15).

It appears that the historical development of counties in Georgia and Florida continues to condition commissioners to act administratively on these two functions, impervious to the relatively recent effects of urbanization and governmental reform. Commissioners from urban and rural counties alike engage more (both legislatively and administratively) in roads and finance matters than in any of the other functions. This heavy involvement, compared to involvement in the non-traditional areas, appears to be a carryover from the time when roads were the primary county business.

Legal constraints placed upon county government by the states also influence commissioners' administrative involvement in certain functions. County government is constitutionally a territorial subdivision of state government, often dating back to the state's creation. As an arm of state government, county government has certain specified functions to perform. In Florida and Georgia, approximately 70 per cent of county budgets are established within the limitations of state statutes.[13] County governments in Florida and Georgia have state-prescribed functions to perform in an administrative framework, even when commissioners sit as a legislative body.

13. Association of County Commissioners of Georgia, "How about Diversified Taxes?" *Georgia County Government Magazine*, April 1972, p. 50.

We hypothesize that the nature of policy roles of commissioners is sufficiently different from city councilmen to warrant analysis. Commissioners govern both incorporated and unincorporated areas, and urban, suburban, and rural areas, and provide both state-mandated and "urban-type" services. The provision of many services has a long-time historical basis, while non-traditional services are being provided in response to the needs and demands of residents. Therefore, we argue that the territorial scope and varying mix of services should indicate caution when comparing county commissioners with city councilmen.

In Table 15, a breakdown of the kind of activity undertaken in carrying out the eight functions is presented. The percentages are representative of the extent to which commissioners engage legislatively and administratively in these activities. Commissioners engage in more administrative than legislative activities for finance (49.8 to 43.5 per cent) and roads (44.3 to 42.3 per cent). The non-traditional functions (in terms of historical development) require more legislative than administrative activity and are generally provided in response to residents' needs and requests. These functions are not necessarily state functions to be "administered" by the county, so that the commissioners can legislate in these newer functional areas free from long-standing administrative responsibilities imposed by the state capital. Thus, the county commissioners "administer" in tandem these traditional activities (roads and finance matters) for the state. There is a high correlation (.90) between commissioners' activity on road and finance functions, substantiating our contention of the historical linkage between these two activities.

County government is still heavily influenced by state control, which means that, for many services, counties have no local option in providing these services.[14] Compared to municipalities, county government is relatively rigid in its structure, and the perceptions of county commissioners reflect this fact. In Table 15, it is suggested that functions without a long historical development (that is, all functions except roads and finance) allow county government commissioners to perceive themselves more as legislators than as administra-

14. Ibid., p. 85. Although cities are also creatures of the state, municipal home rule, in contrast to county home rule, not only confers more freedom to determine organizational structure at the municipal level but also allows the municipality authority to control "local affairs" as distinguished from affairs of "general state interest."

tors. And, in fact, in each non-traditional function, commissioners do engage in higher percentages of legislative than administrative activities.

DECISION MAKING: AGREEMENT-DISAGREEMENT

The analysis of the policy activity of county commissioners will now be extended to a consideration of consensus and non-consensus in decision making. This is important because most commissioners in Florida and Georgia operate without a chief executive. Hence, in most counties, commissioners are not responding to the policy impacts of an executive but rather govern as a committee, not having to react to policy proposals submitted from the "executive branch." Thus, the way commissioners come to agreement or disagreement on issues is a critical component of their policy activities and should be examined. The extent to which commissioners exhibit consensus or division over various issues would provide a strong basis for determining the direction of county policy development.

County commissions function like small committees in making decisions; that is, decisions are based upon majority vote. Commissioners' discussions of issues precede, and result in, a commission decision. For every issue confronting county commissioners, there is a range of agreement and disagreement. Some issues produce no disagreement among the commissioners: commissioners may be in complete agreement either on issues that are relatively unimportant or on issues that are important but where there is no disagreement on the desired course of action. The unimportant issues may include purchase orders or routine administrative matters. An example of the second kind is road maintenance: roads are often maintained according to an agreed-upon plan, with each decision to maintain roads falling within an overall road maintenance policy. A road to be re-surfaced before its scheduled maintenance may cause disagreement among commissioners.

By contrast, it may be more difficult to avoid disagreement among commissioners on issues such as zoning changes which may reflect competing demands from citizens in the community. While some commissioners may be attuned to the interests of developers and real estate interests, others represent those concerned with maintaining the existing character of the community.

There are obviously many reasons affecting the extent to which agreement is achieved among county commissioners in decision making. Here we focus on the extent to which certain conditions produce disagreement among commissioners, two examples of which are the size of the commission and whether an issue involves the county's performing as an administrator for the state or as a local government.

AGREEMENT-DISAGREEMENT ON ISSUES

County commissions are relatively small in both Florida and Georgia, with 74 per cent of the boards having five members. With three exceptions, all Florida counties have five-member commissions. The exceptions are Dade, Duval, and Volusia counties, with eight, nineteen, and nine members, respectively. Fifteen per cent of the commissions in the two states are three-member boards, all of these in Georgia. The largest commission in Georgia is Muscogee County with ten members. Georgia also has twenty-six counties with one-member commissions. (Single-member commissions were excluded from analysis for obvious reasons.) Florida and Georgia commissions (one-, three-, and five-member boards) are relatively small compared to commissions in other states that commonly are composed of more than twenty members and at times as many as one hundred. The size factor, other things being equal (which they hardly ever are), has effects on the extent of agreement-disagreement on issues. We assume that a tendency toward issue agreement among commissioners is related to the size of the commissions. Agreement among commissioners (voting agreement) on issue resolution is the norm on three- and five-member commissions, and across a wide variety of issues, there will be little disagreement. It might be expected that agreement among commissioners would be more difficult to achieve in large commissions, if for no other reason than that there would be more potential for disagreement.

Research on issue resolution indicates that on larger commissions, there is a likelihood that factions may develop which institutionalize disagreement because one faction might vote for an issue and another against it. Although possible, the existence of factions on three-member commissions would be infrequent because one of the factions would consist of only one member against the other two, resulting in social pressure on the dissenter to conform to the majority. The probability of factions and resulting disagreement among commissioners on issue resolution would increase for five-member commissions and would be even greater in seven-member or larger commissions.

The fact that commissioners line up with one another regardless of the content of the specific issues is implicit in our approach to examining agreement-disagreement.[15] This assumption is not unreasonable when applied to very small groups (three and five members) at the local level of government. Following the logic presented by Eulau and Prewitt, we contend that issues facing county commissions are considerably less diverse than those facing state and federal legislative bodies. However, we also contend for reasons discussed in chapter 3 (the urban-suburban-rural split and traditional vs. nontraditional factors) that issues facing counties are more diverse than those confronting cities. In small groups having face-to-face and often close interpersonal relations, stable factionalism despite varying issues is quite likely to result from group pressures to conform to the norms, attitudes, and behavior of those whose respect or help is of value. Moreover we would expect that in a rural setting the shared norms would be even more evident than in small groups in urban settings, where diversity is more readily tolerated.

The size of the commission and level of government are important factors influencing decision making, but obviously other conditions also have impact. The extent to which commissioners approach their jobs professionally and formally supplements the size factor. A formal approach to decision making which relies on research and public hearings is more likely to be found in urban than in rural areas. In slightly urbanized areas, decision making is affected by informal social pressures. Citizens can contact commissioners on a personal basis and request "favors." In more urban areas, population influx into counties ameliorates much of the rural familiarity and social cohesion which can exist between commissioners and constituents. Strangers to a community are not subject to the same amounts of pressure to conform as are long-time friends and neighbors. In urban areas,

15. Eulau and Prewitt, *Labyrinths of Democracy*, p. 173, offer an extended discussion of split voting as it applies to city councilmen in the San Francisco metropolitan area. We have couched our discussion of commissioner agreement in the same context as Eulau and Prewitt have for councilmen. We feel this is consistent with a major theme pursued in this book: to compare cities with counties at every opportunity. After all, much more of the political dynamics of cities is known than of counties, and we feel our understanding of counties will be enhanced by such comparisons. Our argument in this section rests heavily upon the work of Eulau and Prewitt, and we acknowledge their massive contribution to our own effort.

regardless of the commission's size, citizens want decisions according to formalized decision-making procedures, not "favors" likely to be distributed to friends of the commissioners.[16]

Three-member commissions are found in areas which are primarily rural. The norms of rural decision making apply directly to how commissioners approach issues. The rural norm combines and blurs the distinction between social activities and professional decisions on issues made exclusively on their policy and administrative merits.[17] Thus, members of small county commissions are subjected to more informal social pressures than are commissioners on larger governing bodies. On small commissions (three members), the social interaction "spills over" into the formal decision process to a greater extent than, for example, on a seven- or nine-member commission. There is relatively little division of labor on three-member commissions, with all members involved in the total scope of decision activities. There would probably not be committees or sub-committees created to handle specialized tasks when the total commission membership is three.

We have indicated at several points that county commissioners must perform in varying degrees both state administrative tasks and local corporate tasks. The implication of the state-mandated role is that counties are primarily administrative units and that when they act as such, there will be little disagreement in dealing with such issues, whereas more disagreement is likely to be found on issues generated by local corporate demands. Given a long history of functioning as a state administrative sub-unit, counties may not be responsive to citizen requests for services on those issues that may generate disagreement. There may be little disagreement among members in administering state-mandated functions, and a "style" of issue resolution reflecting agreement affects the state-mandated issue areas. The delivery of state-mandated functions has been routinized to the extent that disagreements are not evident at the voting stage. To the extent there are disagreements, they are resolved before they come before the commission for a vote.

The data in Table 16 show that all issues are generally voted on unanimously. Combining the "very often" and "often" categories,

16. See Alvin D. Sokolow, *Governmental Response to Urbanization* (Washington: Economic Research Service, U.S. Department of Agriculture, 1968), chap. 5.
17. Ibid., chaps. 5, 6.

our data show that 89.6 per cent of the commissioners vote unanimously on issues. Only 10.4 per cent said "not very often," and none of the commissioners said that they "never" vote unanimously. We also found a slight tendency toward unanimity existing in larger as opposed to smaller commissions; that is, commission size made little difference in the members' perceptions of unanimous voting. If disagreement exists among commissioners, there is little evidence that it exists at the voting stage of issue resolution.

TABLE 16
COMMISSIONERS' PERCEPTIONS OF EXTENT OF UNANIMOUS
ISSUES AND EXTENT OF DISAGREEMENT ON
NON-UNANIMOUS ISSUES

	Extent of Unanimity on Issues[a]		Extent Same Commissioners Vote Together on Non-Unanimous Issues[b]	
	%	N	%	N
Very often	42.9	(103)	14.8	(35)
Often	46.7	(112)	36.7	(87)
Not very often	10.4	(25)	46.0	(109)
Never			2.5	(6)
Total	100.0	(240)	100.0	(237)

a. The question asked was "How often do the commissioners vote unanimously on issues that are considered?"
b. The question asked was "When commissioners are in disagreement on an issue, how often do the same commissioners vote together?"

Table 16 further illustrates that, among a relatively small proportion of non-unanimous votes, splits involving the same commissioners are infrequent. Only 14.8 per cent of the commissioners indicated that commissioners vote together very often when there is disagreement. Coalitions involving the same commissioners across issues are not evident. Although most commissioners in Florida and Georgia are Democrats, the voting data indicate few identifiable "factions" that band together. A response indicating infrequent voting on issues where there is disagreement does not indicate when voting together does occur. So it is conceivable that voting disagreement occurs infrequently but on the most important issues. Disagreement on a limited number of issues may be significant if the issues themselves are important.

These data, however, do illustrate that commissioners vote unanimously on issues most of the time. If there is disagreement among commissioners, in most cases it does not carry over into the voting stage. Also, when there is split voting, the same commissioners do not vote together; that is, agreement and disagreement at the voting stage appear to be limited to specific issues and not to be the result of some commissioners voting together as a coalition in either a majority or a minority. Although the data are limited, commissioners' banding together across issues to pursue policies was not illustrated. For example, in the five-member commission, a faction of commissioners (one, two, or three in number) does not vote together consistently from one issue to another.

ISSUE AREAS: SPLIT VOTES ON COMMISSIONS

The data in Table 17 set forth the issues which county commissioners indicated were most likely to result in split votes. The commissioners were asked to list no more than three issues. However, most commissioners listed fewer than three, as can be seen from the total of 369 responses (rather than 759). In the broadest sense, Table 17 shows that most commissioners were certain that only one or two types of issues were likely to cause voting splits in their counties. Split voting does not occur on a wide range of issues, and in all probability will occur on only a relatively small number of issues. No single issue was cited by as many as 20 per cent of the commissioners as likely to result in a split vote. This is a dramatic illustration of the infrequency of perceived vote splitting, particularly taking into account the fact that each commissioner had three chances to name issue areas.

The areas of taxes, finances, and budgeting are most likely to produce differences in voting among commissioners. In research on local governments, financial matters have been perennially identified as producing potential disagreement among officials. This suggests that the budget is where fundamental questions of values (policies) are reflected and that budgets are a reflection at the local level of real policy preferences. What is surprising to us is, first, the extent to which there are disagreements among local officials on such matters as tax rates and establishing budgets and, second, that disagreement was not carried into the voting stage of decision making. We are not arguing that county commissioners do not disagree over fiscal matters; in all likelihood they do, but it is resolved or at least contained in the decision-making process before public votes are recorded. Often the disagreements may be hashed out in commission negotiations with administrative agency heads or independently elected administrators.

Although little comparative data exist on the decision-making process of county commissions, we feel that there is pressure for unanimity on voting. It is recognized that, after issues are introduced,

TABLE 17

COMMISSIONERS' PERCEPTIONS ON THE THREE ISSUES MOST LIKELY
TO CAUSE SPLIT VOTES ON COMMISSIONS[a]
(in percentages; numbers in parentheses)

	Florida		Georgia		Combined States	
Taxes, finances, and budgeting	17.3	(32)	20.7	(38)	19.4	(70)
Planning and zoning	23.2	(43)	13.6	(25)	18.4	(68)
Administration, routine personnel	9.2	(17)	21.7	(40)	15.4	(57)
Social and physical services	11.9	(22)	12.5	(23)	12.2	(45)
Roads	10.8	(20)	7.1	(13)	8.9	(33)
Pollution control	16.2	(14)	1.6	(3)	4.6	(17)
Capital expenditures	3.8	(7)	2.7	(5)	3.3	(12)
Other issues (e.g., water supply, recreational development, education, flooding, etc.)	16.2	(30)	20.1	(37)	18.2	(67)
N =		(166)		(224)		(369)

a. The question asked was "On what kinds of issues do the commissioners most likely split their votes? Please list no more than three, if possible."

discussed, and debated, and after compromises are made, disagreements would be resolved before the issues reach the public (voting) stage. What is interesting is that relatively little disagreement (split voting) is evident. The apparent reason is that county commissioners perceive their primary job activity as one of administrative oversight; that is, commissioners are not seeking to be representatives for specific clientele or interest groups. In addition, large portions of county budgets are committed to state-mandated activities (roads, welfare, courts), and often there is little leeway for disagreement on such functions. Further, commissioners in Florida and Georgia are elected at large and geographically represent the entire community, so that relatively few commissioners see themselves as representative of a subgroup (blacks, the poor, businessmen) or sub-areas (suburban or rural) to the extent that they represent that minority's interest continuously across issues. Thus, the pressure of voting for district needs as opposed to the needs of a county-wide constituency is lessened for those commissioners not elected by districts. We do not imply there would be less representation of minority interests, but that such representation is not pursued at the voting stage. There seem to be compromises on issues before the public vote is taken. The fact that counties function as administrative units of the state and that there is an at-large electoral arrangement causes disagreement to be muted at the voting stage.

We recognize that there may be a relationship between the size of the county commission and the population of the county. It appears that larger counties have larger commissions, which would enhance the opportunity of achieving wider-spread representation among the various areas and groups in the county. Even so, the extent to which a commission exhibits voting disagreement may be more a function of county size than of commission size. Generally, larger counties have more diversity and differences of opinion, shown in split voting among commissioners. Unfortunately, we could not examine the relative impact of commission size and county size on the extent of split voting of commissioners. Of Florida's sixty-seven counties, sixty-four have five-member commissions; among the three exceptions, the commissions range from nineteen in the largest to eight in the smallest. In Georgia there was a slight relation between county size and commission size: the larger counties had five-member commissions, the smaller counties had three-member commissions, and the most rural counties had one-member commissions and were excluded from our analysis.

Eulau and Prewitt found that for the San Francisco Bay area, city council size rather than city size seems to engender the possibility of split voting and conflict. They contend that a small group is more capable of establishing harmonious relations in voting while the larger group provides more opportunity for conflict. They classify five members as a small council and seven members as a large council. By contrast, most of the councils that we examined in Florida and Georgia consisted of either three or five members. Thus, by Eulau and Prewitt's definition, we are dealing with small commissions.[18] We contend that the absolute smallness of the commissions (three or five members) overshadowed the distinction in size. We were able to discern no difference between three- and five-member commissions

18. Eulau and Prewitt, *Labyrinths of Democracy*, pp. 74–75, 188.

in the number of split votes. The norm on all commissions in Florida and Georgia was agreement across issues. There was little split voting or continuous factions taking similar sides across issues.

In comparison with municipalities, counties evidence less voting conflict and disagreement. Cities are corporate entities that are created and maintained in response to citizen needs. Citizens make more demands upon cities than upon counties for services, and this factor may result in disagreements. In addition, cities are often structured to enhance representation through district election mechanisms. For example, councilmen who are elected by wards often vote in accordance with their district's preferences, even when these preferences are at odds with those of other councilmen or are likely to result in a minority vote. The corporate status and district representation which apply to cities do not apply equally to counties. Most counties in Florida and Georgia elect commissioners on an at-large basis, and the largest counties use a district election method. As a result, counties exhibit less conflict in decision making than do cities. As noted in chapter 2, counties are coming to resemble the corporate character of cities, and we expect that the decision-making process will likewise be affected, i.e., there will be more disagreement among public officials. Yet, although much as the literature stresses the "changing" role of counties, our analysis of the decision-making process does not confirm many of the current ideas. Counties do not resemble cities in their decision-making style.

A large number, approximately 18 per cent of the commissioners, indicated that planning and zoning issues were likely to result in split votes. In both Florida and Georgia, most growth is occurring in the unincorporated urban fringes. It is the county commissioner who is authorized to respond to requests for zoning changes in these unincorporated areas. High growth in these areas results in requests for zoning changes to accommodate various residential, industrial, and commercial mixes in land use. As indicated by the split vote percentage, these requests often result in disagreement among the commissioners. In a broader context, planning and zoning matters represent a relatively new issue area for county commissioners and fall under the county's newer role as a corporate entity. Zoning and subdivision control are land-use functions that have been the traditional responsibilities of sub-county (municipal) units of local government.[19] Plan-

19. ACIR, *Profile of County Government*, p. 32.

ning and zoning are not state-mandated administrative functions but functions pursued by counties in response to citizen needs at the local level. As late as 1966, twelve states still did not grant counties zoning powers; seventeen others did not confer subdivision powers on counties.[20] Further, the commissioner is the local governor for unincorporated areas, and he cannot avoid decisions that might result in split votes.

In areas where local requests for planning and zoning changes are in conflict, there should be evidence of split voting on county commissions. It would be difficult to obtain consensus on such matters since various groups have opposing zoning interests. Residents want their homes protected from industrial and commercial intrusion; developers and builders often want rural and residential land zoned for development. The potential for disagreement on planning and zoning issues is high, given the adversary nature of requests for zoning changes. That is, a request for zoning is made to the county and advertised publicly to determine if opposition exists.

The argument being advanced here is that as counties assume more city-type functions (such as planning and zoning), decision making will be characterized by more disagreements, for at least two important reasons. First, the county has not routinized planning and zoning administration as it has the more traditional functions such as roads. Counties expend more resources on road construction and maintenance than they do for planning and zoning, yet there is twice as much disagreement on planning and zoning (18.4 per cent) as on roads (8.9 per cent). Counties "administer" roads, and the decision-making process has been regularized, resulting in agreement as to which roads are to be constructed or repaired. Planning and zoning issues may be less amenable to administrative routinization in that the zoning process is characterized by opposing groups and citizens wanting policy decisions in their favor. Moreover, requests for zoning changes are subjected to challenge to determine if such changes will be accepted. Second, as counties provide more corporate-type functions (see chapter 3), they will increasingly function as legislative bodies responding to local needs and demands. This is in contrast to commissions functioning as administrative arms of state government. Commissions *administer* roads, but they *decide* planning and zoning

20. Robert Anderson and Bruce Boswig, *Planning, Zoning and Subdivision: A Summary of Statutory Law in the 50 States* (Albany: New York State Federation of Planning Officials, 1966), pp. 182–85.

matters. This distinction is further dramatized when citizen contact with county commissioners is examined. County commissioners receive more contact from citizens on matters of roads (36.8 per cent of the commissioners stated that they were so contacted) than on planning and zoning (25.1 per cent), yet planning and zoning result in more split votes than do road issues.

MAJOR FUTURE IMPROVEMENT

Having examined how commissioners approach their jobs and the extent of their agreement on issues, we would like now to look at their jobs in the future. Their perceptions will indicate the future

TABLE 18
COMMISSIONERS' PERCEPTIONS OF MAJOR IMPROVEMENT
NEEDED IN COUNTY[a]
(in percentages; numbers in parentheses)

	Florida		Georgia		Total	
Pollution and environmental quality	23.2	(22)	28.7	(35)	26.3	(57)
Roads	20.0	(19)	22.1	(27)	21.2	(46)
Planning and zoning	8.3	(18)	2.8	(6)	11.1	(24)
Provision of physical and social services	3.2	(7)	6.9	(15)	10.1	(22)
Expanding growth and development	5.1	(11)	4.6	(10)	9.7	(21)
Health, education, and welfare	2.8	(6)	5.5	(12)	6.5	(18)
Taxes and finances	.09	(2)	5.5	(12)	6.5	(14)
Limit growth	.05	(1)	0	(0)	.05	(1)
Others	4.1	(9)	2.3	(5)	6.5	(14)
	43.8	(95)	56.2	(122)	100.0	(217)

a. The question asked was "Looking toward the future, what *one* county-wide improvement, in your opinion, does your county need most to be attractive to its citizens?"

shape of county agenda. Will the mix of future issues resemble the current mix, or will the county further evolve into a corporate local government?

The responses in Table 18 indicate which issues will concern county commissioners in the future. The responses indicate that commissioners view the issues both in the traditional county context (roads, welfare) and the corporate context (pollution and environmental quality, planning and zoning, expanding growth and development). The major emphasis of the county's future role is viewed as one of response to local preference and needs as a corporate entity. This is evidenced by the commissioners' first expressed concern, local pollution and environmental quality (26.3 per cent). Their concern with the character of the community is expressed by the perception of the need for better planning and zoning (11.1 per cent). An additional 9.7 per cent of the commissioners indicated that expanding growth and development are the most needed county improvements. These are local issues, and the commissioners respond with the view of the county as a "local" government.

One of the effects of these perceptions of future county needs is that counties will play a role of responsiveness to local needs as well as fulfill the state administrative functions. This "mix" of activities will result in policy involvement on an increasing number of locally generated issues. The provision of increased service delivery will be accompanied by more disagreements among commissioners as to allocation of resources. Priorities among locally generated service requests will be discussed and debated, and frequently disagreement will persist into the voting stage of decision making. The county will increasingly function as a local body as it generates and responds to local demands.

CONCLUSION

The governing processes of counties are in transition. Commissions are functioning more than they have previously as legislative bodies as areas urbanize and as professionally administered services are expected by residents. Although commissioners have a legal mandate from the state to administer services, our data indicate that they do not perceive much administrative involvement in delivering these services. However, the administrative heritage of counties as administrative sub-units of the state persists. The dual role of counties as administrative sub-units and as local governments influences decision making in a manner that makes suspect many comparisons between counties and cities. Counties do not function as cities, even though counties are assuming an increasingly corporate status in response to citizen demands.

Most studies dealing with the legislative-administrative separation focus on municipalities as representative of all local governments. Few studies have dealt with county government as a unit of analysis in examining administrative issues.[21] Although counties exhibit more structure and legal rigidity than municipalities, there appears less distinction between legislative and administrative functions when commissioners' perceptions are examined. Municipal governments have more flexibility and may be less influenced by historical development and state constraints. Viewing the findings of past research on municipalities (in which the literature abounds) as being equally applicable to county governments (which have not been extensively researched) is not warranted. These two units of local government exhibit important differences; both counties and cities merit independent research before generalizations about comparative behavior can be made.

The influences of urbanization and reform on counties appear to go through a rigid historical and legal filter. Counties, unlike cities, were not created in response to the service demands of urban populations. Counties existed long before the impacts of rapid urbanization. Thus, it may not be surprising that the findings of many researchers concerning the consequences achieved by reforming city government are not transferable to counties. This study indicates that reforming county governmental structures does not appear to affect appreciably the legislative-administrative involvement of commissioners. Counties do not have the same characteristics as cities; therefore, generalizations about the effects of city reorganization or urbanization cannot be projected to counties. Counties need separate analysis. Cities have been the focus of a great deal of recent research. The question we raise is how much of this research can be applied to the administrative functioning of counties.

County commissioners tend to approach issue resolution in a unanimous fashion. Little disagreement on any issues exists among the county commissioners. Neither the size of the commission nor of the county was related to vote splitting. What little disagreement that did exist on commissions was found to concern non-traditional issue areas, such as planning and zoning. In sum, the social pressures among commissioners were sufficient to eliminate disagreement and vote splitting. Disagreements were usually resolved informally prior to voting. Whether this pattern of issue resolution will persist as counties grow and evolve into corporate entities remains to be documented.

21. Keith Baker, "Socio-Economic and Political System Change and the Public Policy Process in California's County Government" (Ph.D. diss., University of California, Santa Barbara, 1974), p. 2.

6

Counties as Local Governments: Objectives and Growth

THE amount and type of services delivered by counties have been dramatically increasing. There are diverse issues that commissioners must deal with. Counties are providing more services, particularly in the urban, non-traditional, and social categories. Yet, in a broader sense, a discussion of service delivery does not adequately portray counties as local governments. Counties are undergoing change, and how they respond to public problems is determined by many factors, such as legal restrictions, demands of residents, and the desires of commissioners themselves.

If local governments attempt to reflect the needs and desires of their communities, what objectives do they seek? In this context, the question of what county commissioners want to accomplish is as important as what specific services they are in fact providing and what their legal and resource constraints are. How do commissioners want counties to develop as local governments? What broad objectives do they want counties to achieve?

We will examine here county commissioners' attitudes toward county development, specifically toward these: activities counties should engage in to meet future demands; strategies for dealing with the costs of county services that might be necessary in the future; what improvements are needed to make the county attractive to its citizens. We also examine in detail the perceptions of commissioners toward community growth in their counties. We will argue that the counties' objectives, particularly the critical question of the extent to which commissioners support growth, will have significant impact upon the functioning of county government. Commissioners' evaluations of objectives will influence how governmental structures will be utilized and services selected for delivery.

THE CITY AS A MODEL FOR COUNTY DEVELOPMENT

Cities are often used as a model for county development.[1] City government in the United States has been the main organizational unit for provision of services and general government to localities. As shown in chapter 2, cities were created and developed in response to the service needs of their residents, and they were incorporated where

TABLE 19
CITIES AS A MODEL FOR COUNTY GOVERNMENT:
COMMISSIONERS' PERCEPTIONS[a]
(in percentages)

	Urban Counties	Non-Urban Counties	All Respondents
Agree	87.5	63.4	73.1
Disagree	12.5	36.6	26.9
Total	100.0	100.0	100.0
	(N = 56)	(N = 118)	(N = 242)

a. The question asked was whether "Counties should expand their services just as cities are doing."

population densities stimulated service demands, thus being responsive to urbanization and its effects by providing increased services. As counties have increasingly expanded their services and modernized, the advocates of county government have argued that counties can do everything that cities can.

The data in Table 19 reflect the perceptions of commissioners on a comparison of service delivery by counties with that by cities. Seventy-three per cent of the commissioners indicated that counties should expand their services just as cities are doing, an indication that commissioners see their counties to be in the business of providing services to residents. Thus, cities are not only a basis of comparison for counties but also the model which counties seek to emulate.

The data were broken down on an urban / non-urban basis. An urban county is one having a population of 100,000 or more, and it

1. Banovetz, *Managing the Modern City*, part 3.

is in these that we expect the "pressures" for city-type services to be greatest. The data in Table 19 show that the city is recognized as a service-delivery model for counties by a substantial majority of commissioners from all counties, particularly commissioners from urban counties: 87.5 per cent of the commissioners from urban counties agreed that their counties should expand their services just as cities are doing. The most urban counties are most like cities in their service delivery. Although in the non-urban counties approximately two-

TABLE 20
COUNTY PROVISION OF AMENITIES:
COMMISSIONERS' PERCEPTIONS[a]
(in percentages)

	Urban Counties	Non-Urban Counties	All Respondents
Agree	96.6	91.0	92.3
Disagree	3.4	9.0	7.7
Total	100.0	100.0	100.0
	(N = 58)	(N = 189)	(N = 247)

a. The question asked was if "Every county should provide in its budget for amenities such as parks, libraries, etc."

shaping the growth of their counties? Since a primary function of thirds (63.4 per cent) of the commissioners want to expand services, this proportion was over 20 per cent lower than their urban counterparts.

The data provide a further verification of the extent to which commissioners see the expanded role of the county in providing amenity-type services, such as parks and libraries. The provision of such services is relatively new to counties;[2] cities have traditionally provided service amenities for localities, whereas counties have provided state-mandated services such as roads and court administration. The data in Table 20 indicate that 92.3 per cent of all the commissioners support the provision of amenity services. Although the difference is not large, more commissioners from urban counties (96.6 per cent) than from non-urban counties (91.0 per cent) support such services. Based upon the commissioners' perceptions, counties will be providing the amenity-type services that residents request.

Do county commissioners support land-use controls as a means of

2. Oliver Williams and Charles Adrian, *Four Cities* (Philadelphia: University of Pennsylvania Press, 1963), chap. 9.

shaping the growth of their counties? Since a primary function of cities for several decades has been land-use controls through zoning and subdivision regulations, an answer to this question will provide further insights into how much commissioners want to provide corporate services. Cities have used this important policy mechanism to shape growth and, to a large extent, to determine the character of the population within corporate limits. Some scholars, in fact, have argued that land-use authorities are the most important function cities perform for their residents.[3]

TABLE 21
COUNTY LAND USE POLICY TO CONTROL GROWTH:
COMMISSIONERS' PERCEPTIONS[a]
(in percentages)

	Urban Counties	Non-Urban Counties	All Respondents
Agree	93.1	83.4	85.8
Disagree	6.9	16.6	14.2
Total	100.0	100.0	100.0
	(N = 58)	(N = 181)	(N = 239)

a. The question asked was whether "Counties should utilize strong land control policies to shape the direction of its growth."

The data in Table 21 indicate that 85.8 per cent of all commissioners favor the utilization of strong land-control policies to shape the direction of growth. Similar to the city comparisons, support for strong land-use policies is higher among commissioners from urban (93.1 per cent) than non-urban counties (83.4 per cent). The significance of the data in Table 21 is that land-use control is recognized by an overwhelming majority of all commissioners as a policy to be used by counties to guide growth. The significance of controlling growth in counties may be to stop or to stabilize the current growth rates, or the commissioners' objective may be to stimulate the growth rate of their counties. In either case, the policy implication is that the commissioners recognize that land-use control, which has long been a local policy mechanism of cities, is a legitimate county activity for guiding desired development.

The weight of the data presented in these three tables indicates

3. Daniel J. Elazar, "The New American Town," *Publius* 5, no. 1 (Winter 1975), special issue on *The Suburban Reshaping of American Politics*, ed. Earl M. Baker.

that commissioners see their counties as local governments responding to the needs of urbanized populations. Guiding county growth and providing amenity services are objectives most sought by residents in urbanizing areas. The perspective of pursuing city-type objectives emphasizes quite dramatically the fact that counties, as viewed by the commissioners, are much more than administrative subdivisions of the state. Administering state services is obviously a mandated requirement for counties, but the primary objectives pursued by commissioners extend beyond this to achieving long-range objectives that will transform counties into corporate local entities. In fact, the commissioners use cities as a model for county service delivery activities.

STRATEGIES FOR PROVIDING SERVICES

We will now look at some strategies commissioners rely upon for raising revenues for financing their objectives. We have classified various revenue sources into three broad categories: local revenue sources, revenues to be obtained from non-local sources, and revenues obtained from non-tax sources. By such categorization, we can understand better the constraints and options commissioners perceive for financing broadly based objectives.

Before we discuss revenue-producing strategies, it would be helpful to show where county governments currently obtain their general revenue. The data in Table 22 present major sources of revenue of all county governments in the United States during fiscal year 1973–74. Intergovernmental revenue—almost entirely grants and shared taxes from the states including federal aid channeled through the states—was the largest single source at 44.8 per cent. Part of the intergovernmental revenue reflects county receipts from the federal general revenue-sharing program, which provided county governments with $1.7 billion in 1973–74. County-imposed taxes yield $11.7 billion, 37.9 per cent of all general revenue of county governments. Property taxation was the predominant tax revenue source, supplying $9.6 billion, 31.8 per cent of general revenue. The proportion of total general revenue derived from non-property taxes, e.g., sales taxes, amounted to 6.9 per cent. The proportion derived from charges and miscellaneous sources (e.g., license fees, special assessments, interest earnings, and so on) was $4.7 billion, 15.1 per cent of total revenues.

The data in Table 23 present the commissioners' perceptions of

eight options for raising revenue. These are classified into three categories: resources raised at the local level through taxes and fees of
various kinds; reliance on federal fiscal assistance through grants-in-
aid or revenue sharing; strategies for increasing the tax base by
attracting industry, commercial activities, or high-income-earning
citizens. These eight options represent a perspective on raising reve-

TABLE 22
GENERAL REVENUE FOR ALL COUNTIES IN THE UNITED STATES
IN FISCAL YEAR 1973–74

Item	Amount (millions of dollars)	Per Cent
Revenue from all sources	30,795	100.0
Intergovernmental revenue	13,799	44.8
Revenue from own sources	16,996	55.2
General revenue	16,313	53.0
Taxes	11,662	37.9
Charges and miscellaneous	4,651	15.1
Utility revenue	178	0.6
Liquor store revenue	133	0.4
Employee-retirement revenue	372	1.2

SOURCES: U.S. Bureau of the Census, *County Government Finances in 1973–74* (Washington: U.S. Department of Commerce), p. 1.

nue that differs from the traditional view toward revenue sources that
are utilized by counties. County revenue, traditionally, has come
from property taxes and intergovernmental transfers of funds from
the states and federal government. State aid is distributed to counties
in accordance with formulas which are usually based on variations
of population measures. For example, state aid to counties for education is usually determined on the basis of average daily attendance
in the public schools. State-collected gasoline taxes would be returned
to counties on the basis of gasoline consumed in the county. Obviously, average daily school attendance and gasoline consumption
have a high correlation with population size—generally, the larger
the county, the more children in school and the more gasoline consumed.

The responses were put into four categories, ranging from agreement to disagreement for each of the eight options. The data in
Table 23 illustrate that the commissioners support a multiplicity of

TABLE 23
COUNTY COMMISSIONERS' PERCEPTIONS OF STRATEGIES FOR
DEALING WITH THE COST OF PROVIDING FUTURE SERVICES
(N in parentheses)

Revenue Options	Agree (1)	Tend to Agree (2)	Tend to Disagree (3)	Disagree (4)	Total of Cols. 1 and 2 (5)	Mean Score (6)
Local						
1. Increase property tax rate	3.7% (9)	9.5% (23)	24.4% (59)	62.3% (151)	13.2%	1.3
2. Assess property more closely to market value	36.9% (89)	44.8% (108)	10.8% (26)	7.5% (18)	81.7%	3.1
3. Increase licenses, fees, fines, user charges, etc.	32.4% (79)	37.7% (92)	13.9% (34)	16.0% (39)	70.1%	2.9
Federal						
1. Federal aid: grants-in-aid	35.1% (86)	33.1% (81)	16.7% (41)	15.1% (37)	68.2%	2.8
2. Federal aid: revenue sharing	46.1% (112)	30.9% (75)	14.8% (36)	8.2% (20)	77.0%	3.1
Increase tax base						
1. Attract industrial property	35.2% (81)	35.2% (81)	21.3% (49)	8.3% (19)	70.4%	3.0
2. Attract commercial property	35.1% (86)	35.5% (87)	16.7% (41)	12.7% (31)	70.6%	2.9
3. Regulate influx of residents—zoning	47.0% (116)	30.8% (76)	9.3% (23)	13.0% (32)	77.8%	2.9

N = 247

strategies for raising revenue.[4] The commissioners favor raising taxes locally, relying upon more federal aid, and attracting revenue-producing activities. The property tax and intergovernmental transfers, which currently are the major revenue sources, are only two options among several which commissioners consider.

In fact, increasing property tax to obtain the increased revenue is resisted by the commissioners. Only 13.2 per cent of the commissioners agreed or tended to agree to seek additional resources from property taxes (col. 5). If the property tax should be used to increase revenues, then the total percentage of commissioners favoring this option is less than 4 per cent. The property tax is a revenue source that is sensitive to local pressure: it is a highly visible tax which is presented as a single bill to taxpayers once a year, and property tax revolts among homeowners are not uncommon occurrences for local governments. As commissioners respond in the role of local government, it would appear reasonable for them to seek revenue sources that do not generate great local opposition. The sources of revenue that do not create such opposition are federal aid and expanding the tax base by obtaining tax-producing properties such as industry and expensive residential homes. Few residents oppose getting someone else (e.g., the federal government) to finance county services, although opposition to federal aid may arise if there are "strings" attached. However, strings are more evident when money is spent than when the aid comes as a relief to county taxpayers. The second option—assessing property more closely to market values—is supported by more than a majority (81.7 per cent). The property tax appears to be the most resisted means of raising revenues, although commissioners do consider assessing more closely to market value. In actuality it may be argued that reassessing property value is only another method of increasing the property tax, but technically reassessment of properties is not an increase in taxes. More important, from the perspective of the commissioner, reassessments do not generate the same amount of political opposition as does changing the tax rate.[5]

With the exception of increasing property taxes, all the other options received majority agreement from the commissioners ranging from 68.2 to 81.7 per cent (col. 5). There are some variations in the

4. Robert C. Wood, *1400 Governments* (Cambridge, Mass.: Harvard University Press, 1961).
5. Ibid., esp. last chapter.

extent of seeking resources. For example, more commissioners agree with revenue sharing (77.0 per cent) than with grants-in-aid (68.2 per cent). The commissioners may view more strings attached to grants-in-aid than to revenue-sharing funds. The broad implications of Table 23 are that commissioners seek revenue from a variety of sources (excepting property tax) to support the increasing service delivery activities described in Tables 19–21.

The mean scores (col. 6) illustrate the wide gap which exists between increasing the property tax and all other revenue-producing strategies. The means were computed by assigning a score of one to four across the agree to disagree responses. The mean score for increasing the property tax is 1.3 compared to means that range around 3.0 for all other revenue-producing strategies. In sum, large majorities of county commissioners see their counties as engaging in a wide range of activities and seeking revenues from multiple sources to support these activities. To return to the city-county comparison, the data in Table 23 indicate that there is a similarity between the two types of local government in seeking revenues.

COUNTY COMMISSIONERS: COMMUNITY GROWTH

How and to what extent a county grows affects the objectives it pursues. The availability of resources to finance services is directly related to whether counties are expanding the tax base. Industry is often sought by commissioners because it lessens the tax burdens on residential property taxpayers. However, new industry may bring environmental problems to a county. Air and water quality may be negatively affected by heavy industry, and increased noise may accompany a wide variety of activities, such as amusement parks, which may locate in a county. We will now discuss factors which influence county growth as a context for assessing the impacts of county development.

Growth is usually described by population and economic characteristics. Increases or decreases in county population and accompanying economic changes make growth a multifaceted public issue confronting county commissioners, necessitating governmental action on taxes, land use, zoning, various types of development, and service deliveries. These activities, and the ways in which they affect county growth, are stimulated by many factors in both the public and the private sectors. Growth is not necessarily the result of conscious governmental policy. Rather, the accumulated activities of builders, developers, realtors, corporate executives, and citizens may initiate and shape growth in local areas. County growth or lack of growth usually results from a combination of private activities and—as they are manifested in public policies—public officials' reactions to these activities.

County commissioners have key responsibilities in growth management. They have authority over land-use planning, subdivision regulations, zoning, and the issuance and enforcement of building codes. They also make capital expenditure decisions on roads, sewers, and solid waste and water facilities, each of which directly affects growth. Commissioners potentially have wide influence over growth, and how they perceive growth is a prelude to development.

Commissioners' uses of these authorities provide a critical leverage over local growth, particularly in unincorporated areas, where the potential for growth is greatest. Growth across the nation is occurring on the urban fringes, which are often unincorporated areas under the supervision, regulation, and control of county commissioners.[6] As growth-related problems, such as pollution, land use, subdivision expansions, annexation, overcrowding of schools, and transportation needs, intensify, county commissioners' authorities will be extended. Cities will not have as much leverage over these problems as they have had in the past, because undeveloped land exists almost exclusively in the unincorporated areas which are under county jurisdiction. Therefore, county commissioners are emerging more and more as the public officials whose decisions have the greatest impact on encouraging or stabilizing growth. City officials as well as private individuals and groups will continually need to look to commissioners as key growth decision makers.[7]

We measured Florida and Georgia county commissioners' attitudes toward growth on a scale which ranged from an attitude favoring the promotion of county growth to one favoring the stabilization of county growth.[8] We asked the commissioners if they agreed, tended

6. Oliver P. Williams, *Metropolitan Political Analysis* (New York: The Free Press, 1971).

7. County commissioners' attitudes and thus their potential impact on growth vary across the United States (see pp. 1–2). For a discussion of the importance of counties in the South relative to the nation as a whole, see Wager, *County Government across the Nation*, especially sec. 3.

8. A study of attitudes is an important and legitimate research focus. Policy makers' attitudes are important in all phases of the policy process, particularly

to agree, tended to disagree, or disagreed with seven growth questions which seemed, a priori, relevant. After a factor analysis was made on these seven items, four turned out to be well associated with each other: (1) we should promote county growth and development; (2) we should provide more services to our citizens as a means of encouraging more people to live here; (3) we should stabilize current county growth and development (reverse coded); (4) we should utilize stricter zoning practices to limit growth and development (reverse coded). The final scale had 13 intervals which ran from a low of 4 (most promotion-oriented) to a high of 16 (most stabilization-oriented).[9]

The variables used to explain growth attitudes were urbanization, wealth, governmental complexity, and in which state a commissioner lived. Conceptually, each of these variables is associated with growth.

Urbanization characterizes not only the absolute size of counties but also their changing population dimensions. To capture the dimensions of urbanization, we used population size (1970), population density (1970), the metropolitan/non-metropolitan status of the county (1970),[10] and population change (1960–70) as surrogate indicators of urbanization.

_____

in problem identification and definition. Whether policy is developed in accordance with attitudes is also an important, yet separate, focus of research. The growth attitudes of key policy makers (and, as we have argued, county commissioners are important policy makers on growth matters) deserve separate study and analysis. See the argument on this point by Jones, "State and Local Public Policy Analysis: A Review of Progress" (see p. 11n22).

9. The seven items were subjected to factor analysis to determine if an empirically based unidimensional growth attitude prevailed among the county commissioners. Utilizing a principal factor solution with interactions, the four items that loaded above the .45 level comprised the growth attitude scale. Based upon the results of the analysis, these four items were simply tallied and used as the dependent variable. As a final point of verification, the additive four-item scale correlated with the scale derived from the factor analysis. The additive scale correlated at .99 with the factor analytic scale. With this multiple validation of the growth attitude scale, we were confident that the additive four-item scale and the scale derived from factor analysis were virtually the same. There were three items that did not scale: (1) we should encourage statewide control of county growth and development; (2) we should seek cooperation with adjoining counties in planning for county growth and development; (3) we should allow private landowners to use their land as they see fit for growth and development.

10. If a county was part of an SMSA, we considered it to be in a special and accentuated degree of urbanization. Metropolitanism is considered to be a developed stage of urbanization. See, for example, Campbell, *The States and the Urban Crisis*, chap. 1. See also Vincent L. Marando, "Metropolitan Re-

The relative wealth of a community has been seen as dependent upon growth. A growing community, with increased industry and residences, can provide more jobs and higher wages which, in turn, expand the tax base.[11] The wealth of a county comes from both the collective public wealth and the private wealth of residents. Therefore, we measured county wealth by assessed valuation per capita (1972) and median family income (1970).

The more governmentally complex a county is, the more it must share not only the benefits of growth (e.g., increased tax revenues) but also its problems. County growth may be affected by what other local officials in municipalities and special districts do independently of commissioners' activities. To measure the degree of governmental complexity, we used the total numbers of local governments, municipalities, and special districts in the county (1972).

Are there differences in growth attitudes of Florida and Georgia commissioners which are not explained by urbanization, wealth, and governmental complexity? Growth is a complex, multifaceted issue which results from a number of interrelated public and private activities. For theoretical and practical purposes, we must ascertain whether growth attitudes vary according to characteristics of growth regardless of political boundaries or according to the state in which a commissioner governs. If we find that the state is the dominant influence, then we must refine our concepts and look at past growth experiences and histories and at the interrelationship of a host of variables peculiar to individual states. Practically, the existence of state dominance lends credence to a state approach to solving growth issues.

Our data were derived from interviews with 253 Florida and Georgia county commissioners and from U.S. census information.[12]

search and Councils of Governments," *Midwest Review of Public Administration* 5 (February 1971): 3–15.

11. See Williams and Adrian, *Four Cities*, chap. 9.

12. The 253 commissioners represent 27 per cent of the 938 county commissioners in Florida and Georgia. Three separate mailings of a questionnaire were sent out during the summer of 1972. We did not sample commissioners randomly but sent questionnaires to all Florida and Georgia commissioners. While our responses do not constitute a random sample, we believe the returned questionnaires are representative of the universe of county commissioners. Our data set was compared with the available biographical information kept on record by the Associations of County Commissioners of Florida and Georgia. Although the two associations' records were not completely current and contained some omissions, we felt our sample was not unduly biased along any theoretically important dimensions. See Appendix B.

The attitudes of individual commissioners represent the unit of analysis. Our concern was with the attitudes of individual commissioners representing counties that have certain theoretical characteristics. This distinction is important, since we were concerned with the commissioners' attitudes toward growth, not with the county commissions' policy outputs.[13] We make no inferences about growth policies of county commissioners. Although we do not aggregate individual attitudes into commission attitudes, we do contend that the commissioners' attitudes are important as a predisposition of a policy perspective.[14] If there are significant attitudinal differences among commissioners, we would expect that these differences would affect what they do with respect to growth. This approach allows the resolution of the difficult methodological task of having to aggregate individual attitudes into collective commission attitudes.

EFFECTS ON GROWTH ATTITUDES

In examining the effects of urbanization, wealth, governmental complexity, and state policies on commissioners' attitudes toward growth, we found that the state had the strongest influence. However, before we examine this finding, it is important to discuss the other three, because our data on these variables are suggestive of some interesting patterns about their effects on growth attitudes.

Urbanization.—The data in Table 24 show that commissioners coming from counties which gained population in 1960–70 were more likely to favor stabilization of growth. For example, the data show population change not only as the indicator of urbanization most strongly related to growth attitudes, but also as negatively related to growth. This indicates that past experience with population growth acts as a brake on the commissioners' desire to promote growth in the future. This point is dramatically illustrated when the attitudes of commissioners from counties which had absolute decreases in

13. See Heinz Eulau, *Micro-Macro Political Analysis: Accents of Inquiry* (Chicago: Aldine Publishing Co., 1969). See also Eulau and Prewitt, *Labyrinths of Democracy*, chap. 3.

14. For an analysis of the relationship between attitudes and action, see Herbert C. Kelman, "Attitudes Are Alive and Well and Gainfully Employed in the Sphere of Action," *American Psychologist* 5 (May 1974). See also Harold L. Wilensky and Leon Mayhew, "Why Do They Say One Thing, Do Another?" University Programs Modular Studies (Morristown, N.J.: General Learning Corporation, 1973).

population in 1960–70 are examined. Of our 253 respondents, 60 came from counties which had population decreases in 1960–70. Of these 60 commissioners, 57 (or 95 per cent of those whose counties lost population) expressed attitudes favoring the promotion of growth.

TABLE 24

URBANIZATION, WEALTH, GOVERNMENTAL COMPLEXITY, AND
IDENTITY OF STATE CORRELATED WITH COMMISSIONERS'
ATTITUDES TOWARD GROWTH

	Variable		
	Simple Correlation Coefficient	Multiple Correlation Coefficient	Multiple Correlation Coefficient
Urbanization			
Metropolitan county	.02		
Population size 1970	−.08	.46[a]	
		($R^2 = .21$)	
Population density 1970	−.01		
Population change 1960–70	−.45[a]		
Wealth			
Per capita assessed valuation	−.35[a]	.38	.60[a]
Median family income	−.16[a]	($R^2 = .15$)	($R^2 = .35$)
Governmental complexity			
Total number of local governments	−.29[a]		
Total number of municipalities	−.24[a]	.38[a]	
Total number of special districts	−.32[a]	($R^2 = .15$)	
State			
Florida	−.49[a]		
N = 233			

a. Different from zero at the .05 level of significance.

Contrary to what Eulau and Prewitt found in their San Francisco Bay area study—that population size is the best surrogate indicator of urbanization—we found that the overall effect of urbanization on growth attitudes is primarily a function of population growth.[15] The effects of population size as well as density and metropolitanism, as indicators of urbanization, represent stability. For example, the im-

15. Eulau and Prewitt, *Labyrinths of Democracy*, pp. 67–70.

pact of population size on growth may be relatively minor, since a large county may have maintained its relative size and developed its size over a long period of time. The same stability factor would seem to be apparent for density and metropolitanism.[16] On the other hand, population change embodies size, density, and metropolitanism as relative factors as well as dynamic factors (i.e., increasing). Population change, more precisely population increase, brings more problems. This suggests that the relative value of indicators of urbanization may vary, depending on the phenomena being explained by urbanization.[17] For example, if we had examined attitudes toward local planning, then population size and density might have been more strongly associated than population change. Or if we had examined attitudes toward amenities, then wealth might have been the best predictor.

Wealth.—The data in Table 24 show a moderate relationship between wealth and growth (R = .38). Between the two individual indicators of wealth, public wealth (assessed valuation per capita) had a more significant effect on growth attitudes than private wealth (median family income). In other words, commissioners from counties with a higher assessed valuation per capita were more in favor of stabilizing growth than those from counties with less public wealth. J. Clarence Davies has suggested that a concern for population control is a factor of affluence.[18] Like Davies, our findings suggest that stabilizing growth is a factor of affluence, particularly affluence that can be equated with taxable resources. Personal affluence as measured by median family income does not directly translate into taxable resources for counties. Wealthy people do not necessarily mean wealthy

16. Urbanization can be assessed in both absolute and relative terms. Depending upon how the indicators of urbanization are used, the distinctions in fact may be ambiguous. For example, in this study, population density was used as an absolute measure of urbanization. Yet, population density in Florida and Georgia is low compared to the population densities of cities, particularly the older cities of the Northeast. The most densely populated county in our sample was Pinellas County, Florida, with a population density of 1,971 per square mile. This figure is low compared to the density of Philadelphia (15,903) or San Francisco (15,854). Obviously, caution must be exercised in interpreting the data as well as in assessing what dimensions of urbanization the indicators are tapping.

17. See Han S. Park, "Urbanization and Political Instability" (Paper delivered at the Annual Meeting of the American Political Science Association, September 4–8, 1973, New Orleans, Louisiana).

18. Davies, *The Politics of Pollution* (New York: Pegasus, 1970), pp. 22–23.

counties. A large proportion of a county's taxable wealth may be in the form of industrial or commercial establishments. In many counties, the median family income may be relatively low, yet the county may have a high per capita assessed valuation. The commissioners appear to recognize this distinction. Therefore, affluence insofar as it affects growth takes on a public dimension measured by the total tax base to which a county has access.

TABLE 25
ANALYSIS OF GROWTH ATTITUDE VARIANCE OF COUNTY
COMMISSIONERS BETWEEN AND WITHIN FLORIDA
AND GEORGIA

	Degrees of Freedom	Sum of Squares	Mean Squares	F Ratio	F Probability
Between states	1	502.8	502.8	78.5	0
Within states	247	1582.1	6.4		
Total	248				

State	N	Mean	Standard Deviation	95% Confidence Interval for Mean
Florida	114	7.2	3.0	6.6–7.8
Georgia	135	4.3	2.0	4.0–4.7
Total	249	5.6	2.9	5.3–6.0

NOTE: The higher the mean, the more the attitude represents growth stabilization.

Governmental complexity.—We found that commissioners whose counties were more governmentally complex moderately favored growth stabilization ($R = .38$). This suggests that where growth is divided among many local governments, its positive effects on tax resources are shared. Municipalities and school districts within a county can lay claim to a portion of the wealth generated by population growth. Consequently, commissioners are aware that the positive economic aspects of growth are not solely at the disposal of the county. On the other hand, negative aspects of growth, such as traffic congestion and pollution, are not neatly packaged among the local governments. These negative consequences "spill over" local governments and affect them all.

State differences.—The state in which a commissioner resides was found to be a stronger indicator of growth attitudes than urbanization, wealth, and government complexity $(R = -.49)$. How then do growth attitudes of Florida and Georgia commissioners differ? We found Florida county commissioners to be oriented more toward stabilizing growth and Georgia county commissioners to be oriented more toward promoting growth. As the data in Table 25 show, on

TABLE 26
MEAN ATTITUDES TOWARD GROWTH AS A FUNCTION OF
STATE AND ACTUAL POPULATION CHANGE 1960–70

County Population Change, 1960–70	Florida Mean	Georgia Mean
Lost population	6.00	3.77
	$(N = 7)$[a]	$(N = 53)$
Gained 0–25% population	5.76	4.66
	$(N = 45)$	$(N = 66)$
Gained more than 25%	8.37	4.88
population	$(N = 62)$	$(N = 16)$[a]
State mean	7.19	4.34
Total N	114	135

	F-Ratio	Significance Level
State	29.77	.001
Population change	44.75	.001
Interaction state		
× population change	4.51	.05

NOTE: The higher the mean, the more the attitude represents growth stabilization.
a. The large discrepancy of all sizes (N = 7 vs. N = 16) reflects the fact that Florida has grown very rapidly (37 per cent) during the decade 1960–70 and relatively few counties lost population, whereas Georgia had moderate growth during the decade (16 per cent) and approximately a third of its counties lost population.

the 13-interval attitude scale, the mean score for Florida commissioners was 7.2, for Georgia commissioners, 4.3. Moreover, these data show that this variation in growth attitudes is accounted for by the differences between Florida and Georgia rather than by the differences within each state.

Since county growth rate (1960–70) and state growth rate were the two variables most strongly related to growth attitudes, are the differences between Florida and Georgia commissioners' attitudes toward growth attributable to differential growth rates in the two states? As shown, commissioners from growing counties in both states expressed support for stabilizing growth to a greater extent than did commissioners from slower-growing or no-growth counties (see Table 26).

Not only do past experience with growth and the home state of a commissioner both influence attitudes, but these two variables may interact. We examined the relationship between county population change and growth attitudes for each state separately; then we examined the interactive effects of both variables upon growth attitudes. The simple correlation coefficients indicate that population change is negatively related to promotion of growth attitudes in both Florida ($-.39$) and Georgia ($-.22$). Although population change accounted for more than three times the variance in Florida (15 per cent) than in Georgia (5 per cent), the difference only approached significance ($p = .07$).

CONCLUSION

The overwhelming implication of data presented in this chapter is that commissioners view counties as local governments and as much more than administrative subdivisions of the state. Commissioners feel that counties should deliver a wide range of services to their residents, both those services that the county has traditionally provided, such as roads and court administration, and those that are considered amenities, such as parks and libraries. Responsiveness to citizens' needs provides the stimulus to the counties' increasing involvement in a wide range of services. This test of responsiveness to citizens is what qualifies counties as local governments: the state is not mandating counties to provide a comprehensive package of services.

One of the major findings is that the commissioners themselves view cities as the appropriate model by which counties should develop. That is, most commissioners stated they wanted their counties to expand services just as cities are doing. In fact, commissioners from all counties overwhelmingly preferred the city as a service delivery model for counties (see Table 19).

The commissioners also recognize that providing more services means an increased need for revenues. They agreed with several options for raising revenues that have not been traditionally relied upon by counties: they supported attracting more industry and commerce and agreed to more reliance on fees and greater acceptance of federal aid. Property tax increases were the only revenue source they resisted. The major implication of these attitudes is that county commissioners will rely upon many revenue sources for the expanded services that counties will provide. This relationship between revenues and services is a further indication that, from the commissioners' perspective, counties are comprehensive local governments.

We examined the growth issue in a demographic framework (size of county, population change in 1960–70, and so on). We hypothesized that the commissioners from the more urban counties would be most resistant to growth, but this belief was not supported. Surprisingly, the most powerful explanatory variable on the commissioners' attitudes toward growth was the state of residence. Florida commissioners, regardless of size of county, resisted growth more than Georgia commissioners did. The historical experience with rapid growth in Florida continues to exert a slow-growth attitude even on commissioners from non-urban counties and counties that did not grow during the 1960s.

The issue of growth and development illustrates the variation of attitudes that existed among commissioners. Had we conducted our study in the 1950s or 1960s, we might have obtained nearly unanimous support for continued growth among the commissioners. But the 1970s have brought a reassessment of growth by the public, as well as by many county commissioners. The issue of growth is being assessed for costs and benefits by many commissioners, particularly those in Florida, and this will have impact on counties' objectives for years.

Our assessment indicates that the state in which a county is located is critical for understanding local officials' attitudes, and this factor raises a number of questions concerning the study of local government. The state provides a context for local governments, but this context is broader than just the state's provision of certain legal and fiscal boundaries. State statutes, such as home rule and financial support of county government, are important and influence attitudes of local officials. However, depending upon the issue under investigation, the impact of state policies on counties may be both subtle and dramatic. Florida has provided its counties with more state policies on growth than has Georgia. The examination of growth presented here was indicative of this state-related impact.

Analysis of the development of counties as local governments is an emerging field of inquiry. This preliminary study indicates that the state within which counties function must be considered for its independent influence on local policies. Analysis of local governments can most effectively be pursued in a framework which takes into accord variations among states. Counties, or for that matter all local governments, are part of an intergovernmental service delivery network which includes the state and federal governments.

7

The Forgotten Governments in Transition

A perspective on how county commissioners respond to public problems and how urbanization and state and federal activities influence responses to these problems has now been developed. A central element of the analysis has been commissioners' perceptions of issues, responsibilities, policy roles, decisional consensus, and service deliveries. How commissioners perceive issues and policy activities is important in determining how county governments respond to public problems.[1]

Many county decisions are made within the context of a changing environment and are shaped by state and federal authorities. Urbanization, for example, was shown to effect county responses to public problems in several important ways. First, while urban counties offer many more services than do non-urban counties, both generally provide the same array of services, particularly those which deal with promotion and development, social and remedial, and governmental and administrative activities. Urban and non-urban counties differ most on functions legislating the activities of residents and requiring the provision of utility services. Second, urban more often than non-urban counties have professional administrators. Third, urban county commissioners pursue a broader range of strategies in responding to public problems than do their non-urban counterparts.

The state continues to exert a strong influence over county activities. State constitutions and statutes establish many of the organizational and policy options open to county commissioners. In Florida

1. For a discussion of attitude research on local government see Jones, "State and Local Public Policy Analysis: A Review of Progress."

and Georgia, as well as across the nation, separately elected county officials are mandated by state constitutions (e.g., sheriff, tax assessor). These offices can be eliminated or their major functions altered only through state constitutional revision.

The impact of the state on counties goes beyond what is written into state constitutions. For example, in analyzing Florida and Georgia commissioners' attitudes toward growth, we suggested that cultural and political experiences of states permeate local issues. Florida commissioners were found to support growth for their counties to a significantly lesser extent than Georgia commissioners. The reason is not to be found in constitutional differences between the two states, but in past growth experiences with urbanization, the policy activities of private and government officials at the state and local levels, and the current attention given to growth in each state.

In recent years, federal programs have continually had more and more influence on how county officials respond to county issues. Federal grant-in-aid programs in areas such as law enforcement, air quality control, and community development have expanded existing county programs or allowed counties to create new programs where none previously existed. Federal programs have made new resources available to counties to offer a wide range of traditional as well as non-traditional programs. In some cases, federal grant-in-aid programs have altered the priorities of county commissioners by making funds available for services they might not have otherwise provided (e.g., air quality control).

Revenue sharing has also bolstered the provision of services by counties. For one thing, revenue-sharing funds provided counties with approximately 6 per cent "extra" funds in 1973–74, thereby increasing their capacity to provide services. As a Brookings Institution study has shown, revenue-sharing funds have relatively greater impact on poor counties than on counties with higher resident income.[2] Thus, revenue sharing along with other federal programs will continue to have a significant impact on the policy options of county commissioners.

PERCEPTIONS AND POLICY

The literature on counties is almost exclusively concerned with descriptive assessments of the legal and organizational structures of

2. Nathan et al., *Monitoring Revenue Sharing*, p. 128.

counties and the extent of service delivery.[3] Most county studies are
also quite normative in their plea for the need for greater authority
of counties to raise revenue and provide services. We have departed
from the traditional direction of research on counties by focusing on
commissioners' perceptions. We have used legal and structural attributes of counties as well as their socioeconomic and demographic
characteristics to examine the context of commissioners' responses
to public problems.

Much of the literature on local governments extols the virtues of
"modernizing" counties by appointing a professional manager or by
having an elected executive.[4] In examining what commissioners perceive to be their legislative and administrative policy activities, we
found their activities to be little affected by the existence of a county
manager. We would not infer from this finding that a professional
county manager has no effect on county policies, but we should not
expect extensive changes in county policy responses merely by hiring
one. As indicated, commissioners perceive a very different policy
world than organizational charts suggest.

It is important to determine what functions the state requires of
counties, but a legal analysis neither captures what commissioners
do within the scope of their authority nor indicates why and when
they take policy initiatives. In Florida and Georgia, counties are
legally restricted from levying personal income or sales taxes, but
commissioners in both states were found not to be particularly concerned with the absence of these revenue sources. They indicated
strong support for other revenue options, such as increased property
assessments, encouraging industry to locate in their counties, and
increased revenue-sharing funds. Florida and Georgia commissioners
were also found to resist increasing property taxes. Although arguments have been made for using sales and income taxes as alternatives to property taxes, our study suggests that commissioners in these
states do not view sales and income taxes as viable alternative revenue sources.

Since Florida and Georgia do not allow counties to levy personal
income taxes and sales taxes, the major sources of revenue for counties are the local property tax and federal and state transfer of funds.

3. Duncombe, *County Government in America.*
4. ACIR, *The Challenge of Local Governmental Reorganization* (Washington: ACIR, 1974), 3:164–65.

This tax structure has an impact on counties' activities and on their capacity to respond to public problems. What occurs at the state level sets the context for counties to respond to the requests and needs of residents. Counties are linked legally and fiscally with the state government.

The relationship between commissioners' perceptions and the legal framework within which commissioners operate is further illustrated by county activities on road construction and maintenance. All counties in Florida and Georgia must provide road construction and maintenance. Whether or not commissioners perceive roads to be an important issue, whether or not urban commissioners feel roads are more important than non-urban commissioners do, and whether or not commissioners feel they should assume the bulk of responsibility for roads or share that responsibility with other governments are important dimensions of county responses to road construction and maintenance which are not revealed by an examination of the legal framework. Both urban and non-urban commissioners in both states were in agreement about roads as a county issue. There was little conflict on how this service should be provided. Yet, road expenditures constitute a major budget item in all counties. Thus, the extent of expenditures and state mandates to provide road services does not capture all dimensions of county road construction and maintenance policy.

SERVICES AND INTERGOVERNMENTAL RELATIONS

More and more demands are being made on counties for increased levels of services. Residents everywhere want increased and more professionally administered county services. This is particularly the case in the urbanized areas in terms of absolute measures.[5] Although non-urban counties do not perform services with as much frequency as urban counties, non-urban counties perform the same type of services.

What we have emphasized is not the fact that service demands are increasing but the pattern by which Florida and Georgia counties provide services, particularly service delivery within the state-county

5. National Association of Counties, *National Survey of the Appointed Administrator in County Government* (Washington: National Association of Counties, 1973).

financial context. There are not enough resources to deal with all demands for services. On almost all the issues considered in this study, commissioners' perceptions of responsibility are intergovernmental, particularly on those issues that are mandated by state or federal laws. However, commissioners' perspectives on issue responsibility are extremely complex, varying from issue to issue. For example, commissioners feel they should assume a greater share of responsibility over those issues on which they can exercise independent authority (e.g., planning, zoning).

By examining counties in an intergovernmental setting, we assessed how the activities of counties are affected by the policies of other local governments as well as by the state and federal governments. States provide the legal setting and many of the fiscal resources of counties. In addition, state legislatures have the authority to grant counties supplemental sources of revenues and increased home rule to respond to public problems without counties having to obtain new laws each time a request is made for policy outside their existing authority. The federal government has expanded financial support to counties both through grant programs to deal with specific problems and through revenue sharing. City policies, such as zoning and tax decisions, often directly affect county areas by increasing county population. Decisions by city officials which increase population intensify the service needs and demands of citizens in both the city and the county. All city residents are also county residents. They pay taxes and receive services from both local units. Yet issues such as growth and development do not come neatly packaged to a city or to the unincorporated portion of a county. Population growth spills across local boundaries, often requiring interlocal policy responses to the service needs of residents.

Research on county governments has not taken into account how commissioners operate in an intergovernmental context. Our analysis has shown that counties cannot be examined adequately without recognition of the intergovernmental context in which they function. Assessment of county law and organization structures is not sufficient focus for analysis of county government. Increasingly, an analysis of a single level of government, whether county, city, state, or federal, will be approached in part as an intergovernmental analysis. The legal and policy linkages among the various governments are too consequential in their impact to be excluded when analysis focuses on one level of government.

COUNTIES: DEVELOPING LOCAL GOVERNMENTS

Counties in Florida and Georgia, as well as throughout the nation, function along two basic dimensions. First, counties continue to operate in their traditional role of administrative subdivisions of the state, the county being the local delivery mechanism through which the state provides its services. Some of the primary services all counties provide in this capacity are road construction and maintenance, administration of the lower courts, law enforcement through sheriffs' departments, recording vital statistics (e.g., births, deaths, auto registration), welfare administration, and administration of elections. Although some variations in both quality and quantity of these services exist, the state mandates these functions to all counties and exerts close supervision by providing funds and establishing regulations.

Second, counties are developing into corporate entities similar in many respects to municipalities.[6] They are responding to the demands of local residents for specialized services. Generally speaking, corporate local governments are empowered by the state to set forth their jurisdictional boundaries, governmental functions, structure and organization, methods of finance, and election and appointment of officers and employees. The consequence of corporate status is to obtain the powers of local self-government for responding to community needs and demands. Wide variation exists among counties with regard to the quality and extent of professionally administered services, but in most counties there is evidence of provision of corporate services. Counties perform functions which cover a wide range—from amenities to economic development to regulations and controls to social welfare. Those functions which counties provide as local corporate governments have been identified by some researchers as "urban services."[7] Our study has basically supported this contention. We found that both urban and non-urban counties do provide city-type services and function as corporate entities. In fact, as we have indicated, many non-urban counties are providing this type of service.

6. We are using municipality corporations as a model to illustrate some dimensions of change within counties. Counties will not become cities. All the powers extended to cities will not be assumed by counties. For example, changing local boundaries among counties must be performed by the state, and often this would require a constitutional amendment. Our major point is that counties are coming to resemble cities in their capacity to respond to strictly local demands.

7. National Association of Counties, *From America's Counties Today.*

The evaluation of counties as corporate local governments has had a legal parallel in the movement for home rule for counties.[8] The intended effect of home rule is to reverse "Dillon's rule" and enable counties to pursue policies not prohibited by the state constitution or by statute. In other words, home rule would legally expand a county's ability to perform corporate functions as long as it was not prohibited from doing so by the state. As with municipalities, through home rule the state would empower a county to enact policies in response to local demands. A county home rule charter would allow county commissioners to enact "local policies" in much the same way that municipal governing bodies establish policy by enacting ordinances.

Our analysis has shown that commissioners in Florida and Georgia view their counties as corporate entities even though most counties have not chosen to adopt home rule status where that option is available. Although the laws of Florida and Georgia may not say that counties are corporate entities, commissioners perceive their counties as similar to cities. We contend that when counties adopt home rule in Florida and Georgia, it will conform to commissioners' current perceptions.

CITY AND COUNTY DIFFERENCES

While counties as corporate local governments are beginning to resemble municipalities, several major distinctions still exist. Counties continue to be a hybrid form of local government, operating both as state administrative sub-units and as corporate local governments. Cities are primarily corporate entities created in response to local needs, and states do not require them to function as administrative sub-units. Further, when compared with cities, counties do not have the same degree of financial latitude and are under more restrictive limits on amounts and types of tax options. Even though counties, because of their larger geographic areas, are in a better position to move away from dependency on the property tax and to utilize other taxes, they have not done so. Presumably, lack of county home rule and of sufficient state enabling legislation has kept them from further diversifying their revenue sources.

8. Home rule charters are designed to give counties the power to adopt governmental structures and provide county services, as they see fit, without state legislative interference.

We have compared counties with cities, but in only two states under a limited set of conditions. We have made a small beginning in comparing the policy contexts and responses of counties and cities and have presented some initial and limited findings. More broadly based comparative assessments of counties and cities need to be made. Our findings suggest that we should exercise caution in applying to counties the results of research on cities. Almost exclusively, the city has served as the unit of analysis in studies on local general governments (exclusive of school districts or special districts). In fact, the popularized accounts of urban politics, urban policy, or "urban crisis" refer to city politics, city policy, or the "crisis" of the cities.[9] Right now, in contemporary America, "urban" may in many cases be equated to "city." However, urban is not yet accepted as a surrogate for county. This research does not allow us to view the dynamics of city politics and problems as analogous to county politics and problems.

Counties differ from cities in several important respects. Counties are a higher level of government than cities. They encompass cities territorially, but cities do not encompass counties.[10] With one exception nationally, and with no exceptions in Florida and Georgia, counties encompass and include cities, often many cities, within their territorial jurisdictions. For example, Dade County, Florida, has 26 cities within its boundaries and Fulton County, Georgia, has 13. However, Florida and Georgia counties are not as complex governmentally as counties in some other states, for example, California, Illinois, and Pennsylvania. In Allegheny County (Pittsburgh), Pennsylvania, there are 84 municipalities.

City residents are also county residents. By contrast, county residents in unincorporated areas do not reside in a city. County commissioners, therefore, govern federal republics in "miniature." Commissioners must also operate as middlemen between state and city on many activities. Commissioners must administer state services to city residents. In addition, they must coordinate many services, such as law enforcement and road construction, which overlap city boundaries.

Counties have a more inclusive mix of urban and suburban popula-

9. Edward Banfield, *The Unheavenly City Revisited* (Boston: Little, Brown, 1973), pp. 3–4; Robert L. Lineberry and Ira Sharkansky, *Urban Politics and Public Policy* (New York: Harper & Row, 1974), epilogue.

10. New York City is the only exception, being composed of five boroughs (counties).

tions than do cities. Counties include cities and suburbs, but, by definition, cities, particularly central cities, do not include suburbs.[11] The common pattern of governmental development in urban areas is that of a large central city surrounded by suburban municipalities. Unlike the county, a single city government does not have a territorial scope to govern the core area and the suburban fringe. More dramatically, county government in Florida and Georgia includes rural areas as well as cities and suburbs. This is illustrated by Dade County, Florida, which is both the most urban county in the state and the largest agricultural producer as well. Dade (Miami) and Duval (Jacksonville) counties, Florida, and Fulton (Atlanta) County, Georgia, not only have populations approaching one million, but also include small towns, farms, and rural areas. The significance of this population "mix" (city, suburbs, rural) of counties is that they are subjected to a wider array of demands than are cities. Few, if any, cities in the United States are confronted with requests for livestock inspection, agricultural extension programs, fish and game management, or soil conservation services. Even the smallest counties provide these services. Counties in most cases must be attuned to the demands of rural and agricultural interests as well as urban and industrial interests.

The array of demands confronting commissioners is relatively wide when compared with cities' needs. County commissioners must be attentive to the demands of core city residents (often minority and poor), suburban residents (often white and middle-income), and rural residents (often farmers). How the different mix of populations between counties and cities affects the functioning of these units should be a subject of continued analysis.

The application of research findings on counties and cities is further complicated by the fact that counties are the only local governments for sizeable portions of their residents. The residents of unincorporated areas are governed locally by the county commission. By contrast, residents of cities are governed locally by both city councils and county commissions. Where the populations of cities and unincorporated areas differ, we would expect the demands and the subsequent response of local government to differ also. Most of the residents of the suburban fringe of urban areas in Florida and Georgia live in unincorporated areas. Suburban residents are more likely to be white, middle-income, highly educated residents with

11. Edward Banfield and James Q. Wilson, *City Politics* (Cambridge, Mass.: Harvard University Press, 1973), pp. 33–46.

different expectations of and demands on local government than those of central city residents. These suburban residents make their demands directly to county government. On the other hand, city residents are members of minority and low-income groups who make their primary demands upon city government. Thus, counties are directly confronted with the demands of suburban (unincorporated) residents, while cities serve as a buffer for them when they must respond to city residents. Although we did not examine the issue, we suspect that residents of unincorporated suburbs have a greater impact on counties than their numbers indicate. The differences among cities and counties as they affect residents in terms of representation, problem identification, and policy responses warrant intensive research.

In many cases, counties are becoming the new suburban form of local government. Murphy and Rehfuss indicate that "most major central cities are now locked in by annexations of suburban municipal governments. This situation has created a need for county governments to provide 'city-type' services in the unincorporated areas as well as to supplement the services provided by small suburban jurisdictions."[12] The ever increasing suburban population which relies directly upon counties as local governments accounts for this observation.

The cities, especially the central cities, by contrast, are the recipients of the urban crisis.[13] It is the central cities which are most seriously confronted with the problems of poverty, inadequate education facilities, segregation of minorities, and crime. Crime statistics, especially violent crimes, indicate it is a central city problem, not a county-wide problem, even in the most urbanized areas.

In the suburbanizing areas, the primary problems are not crime or poverty related issues but those involving amenity services (parks, libraries, and so on) and development and community growth.[14] Growth in urban areas is at the suburban fringes under county jurisdiction and authority. Twenty-six of the largest and most rapidly growing counties in the nation are strictly suburban counties with

12. Murphy and Rehfuss, *Urban Politics in the Suburban Era*, p. 147.
13. Fred R. Harris and John Lindsay, *The State of the Cities* (New York: Prager Publishers, 1972), pp. 3–7.
14. See Banfield, *The Unheavenly City Revisited*. We do not argue here that suburban and rural areas are without poverty or crime. Our emphasis is that central cities are confronted proportionately with more of the problems that have come to be associated with the urban crisis.

no major central city.[15] County commissioners are confronted directly with growth and must respond to growth and development problems to a greater extent than they do to problems of the central city.

URBANIZATION AND COUNTIES

There is little evidence to suggest that the county will be the new metropolitan governmental structure for urban America. The frag mented, decentralized political landscape will more than likely remain. Along with counties, there will continue to be a multiplicity of other local governments (cities, townships, special districts, and school districts). However, counties have some attributes—territorial pervasiveness and action as administrative sub-units of the state— which affect their political status in an urbanizing society.[16]

The political status of county governments in an urbanizing society is also related to the population characteristics and changes within their jurisdictions. The relationship of population to county government is illustrated by two basic factors. First, American society is metropolitan: approximately 70 per cent of the population lives in 270 metropolitan areas throughout the country. The proportion of persons living in metropolitan areas is increasing. Metropolitanization is a condition that is profoundly affecting all citizens. Even persons living in rural areas are assuming urban life-styles. This has been stimulated by society's utilization of technology, particularly in the form of mass communication and transportation.[17] Many persons living in non-metropolitan areas commute to the urban centers for employment.

The manifestation of these characteristics of urbanization on counties takes several forms. All counties are increasing the number of services they provide. Although minor cutbacks in services may occur, particularly in times of economic contraction, the overwhelming trend is in the direction of expanded public services. Reformers interested in illustrating the responsiveness of counties to citizen demands point out this trend. However, the fact is that all governments, cities, townships, special districts, state governments, and the federal government are also increasing the number and types of services delivered. The expenditures of all governments are increasing to pay for those serv-

15. Murphy and Rehfuss, *Urban Politics in the Suburban Era*, p. 146.
16. Willbern, *The Withering Away of the City*, pp. 9–34.
17. Williams, *Metropolitan Political Analysis*.

ices. The critical issue concerning counties is not that they will provide
more services but rather what services will be provided, what processes will be involved, and which services will have priority. Conditions may dictate that commissioners emphasize law enforcement or
environmental and recreational services over welfare or road construction. We have indicated several factors which affect county response to public problems through service delivery. We have indicated
that adequate discussion of county service delivery must take place
in an intergovernmental context. One of the crucial factors to be
assessed is how all governments in their combined efforts respond to
the demands of citizens, not whether counties are providing more
services.

County reformers also take delight in pointing out that county
government is modernizing.[18] The trend toward modernization is
documented by showing the dramatic increase in the adoption of the
county administrator plan among counties, and this also indicates
that county officials now are more professionally trained and have
higher competency than their predecessors. It has been our contention
that professionalism is a response to the increasing demands of urban
life-styles which affect all governments. Are there any governments
which are less professionally administered now than in the past? We
doubt that there are. The issue we have identified as critical is the
relationship of service delivery to the resolution of public problems.

A second factor of the metropolitanization of counties is the dramatic changes which are taking place in population size and characteristics. How counties are adapting to these changes has not been
clearly assessed. Two interrelated phenomena are most often cited as
the fundamental forces of population change affecting counties. One
is the "sorting out" of both population and economic activities between city and suburban county areas and among suburbs. Residents
of the central city are generally poorer and less educated than most
suburbanites. Second, suburban areas are not homogeneous: there
are suburbs which are industrialized with predominantly poor minority groups, as well as the white, middle-income groups. Moreover,
the central city is increasingly losing economic activities to suburban
areas, in most cases relatively and in many cases absolutely.

Another force often mentioned is the highly decentralized system
of local governments in urban areas. Local governmental jurisdic-

18. See Duncombe, *County Government in America.*

tions govern only portions of metropolitan areas. Cities of urban areas often govern populations with widely differing characteristics. There are likely to be local jurisdictions made up of the wealthy and of the less affluent. No single local urban area in the United States is governed by a single local governmental unit which is responsive to the needs of all residents of the metropolitan area.

Primarily because it is a territorial unit with sufficient geographic scope, the county is increasingly being championed as the unit of local government to which urban populations should turn for resolution of pressing urban problems. York Willbern recognized the relationship of urbanization and county government: "The territorial units [counties] must certainly be a major component of a new model. Since they cover all of the land, they are always available to regulate or to provide service to a citizen wherever he may live. . . . Great variations will occur, of course, from state to state, even within a state, but it seems likely that increasingly the center of responsibility for performing a great range of local governmental activities will gradually be shifted from cities to counties."[19]

How counties are responding to public problems, and why their responses take the form that they do, are now being recognized as important questions. However, an adequate assessment of the conditions and factors affecting the urban county's ability to respond to pressing problems is muddled by reformers who contend, without sufficient evidence, that the county is the logical unit of local government to respond to urban problems. This logic is often not supported by empirical analyses of how counties function. Our analysis at a minimum has illustrated that counties are a hybrid form of local government, dependent in many areas for direction on other units and levels of government. We conclude that counties are undergoing change in response to public problems and that this change needs to be examined empirically in order to determine its causes and consequences. At present, too much of what we know about counties is based on "logic" and on the reform ethic, not research. The reform ethic surrounding counties needs to be tested and the political processes of counties systematically researched.

19. Willbern, *The Withering Away of the City*, pp. 119–20.

Appendix A

Profile of Florida and Georgia
County Commissioners

TABLE A.1
PLACE OF BIRTH
(in percentages)

	Florida Commissioners	Georgia Commissioners	Urban Commissioners	Non-Urban Commissioners	All Commissioners
In state presently serving as commissioner	57.8	92.5	67.9	79.6	76.9
Not in state presently serving as commissioner	42.2	7.5	32.1	20.4	23.1
In county presently serving as commissioner	40.2	57.3	35.7	53.5	49.0
Not in county presently serving as commissioner	59.8	42.7	64.3	46.5	51.0

TABLE A.2
PRESENT RESIDENCY
(in percentages)

	Florida Commissioners	Georgia Commissioners	Urban Commissioners	Non-Urban Commissioners	All Commissioners
City	16.8	14.8	40.4	8.4	15.7
Suburb	14.2	13.3	35.1	7.3	13.7
Small town	36.3	28.1	10.5	38.2	31.9
Rural area	13.3	12.6	7.0	14.7	12.9
Farm	19.5	31.1	7.0	31.4	25.8

TABLE A.3
LENGTH OF RESIDENCY
(in percentages)

Years	Florida Commis- sioners	Georgia Commis- sioners	Urban Commis- sioners	Non- Urban Commis- sioners	All Commis- sioners
10 or less	6.4	2.2	3.6	4.2	4.1
11 to 25	23.6	13.4	25.0	16.0	18.0
Over 25	70.0	84.3	71.4	79.8	77.9

TABLE A.4
EDUCATION ATTAINED
(in percentages)

	Florida Commis- sioners	Georgia Commis- sioners	Urban Commis- sioners	Non- Urban Commis- sioners	All Commis- sioners
Less than high school	15.3	24.4	8.9	23.7	20.3
High school degree	29.7	25.2	19.6	29.5	27.2
Trade school	0.9	3.0		2.6	2.0
College—incomplete	18.0	20.0	23.2	17.9	19.1
College—degree	23.4	15.6	19.6	18.9	19.1
College—graduate work	12.6	11.9	28.6	7.4	12.2

TABLE A.5
OCCUPATION
(in percentages)

	Florida Commis- sioners	Georgia Commis- sioners	Urban Commis- sioners	Non- Urban Commis- sioners	All Commis- sioners
Farmer/rancher	27.3	31.6	12.3	34.9	29.7
Professional	7.3	13.2	14.0	9.5	10.6
Businessman	36.4	39.7	49.1	34.9	38.2
Salesman	4.5	3.7	1.8	4.8	4.1
Full-time county commissioner	19.1	8.8	21.1	11.1	13.4
Other	5.5	2.9	1.8	4.8	4.1

TABLE A.6
RETIRED FLORIDA AND GEORGIA COMMISSIONERS
(in percentages)

	Florida Commissioners	Georgia Commissioners	Urban Commissioners	Non-Urban Commissioners	All Commissioners
Yes	14.4	9.0	10.7	11.7	11.5
No	85.6	91.0	89.3	88.3	88.5

TABLE A.7
POLITICAL EXPERIENCE
(in percentages)

Have You Held Other Political Offices?	Florida Commissioners	Georgia Commissioners	All Commissioners
Yes	26.8	25.4	26.0
No	73.2	74.6	74.0

TABLE A.8
POLITICAL AMBITIONS
(in percentages)

Do You Plan to Seek Any Other Public Offices?	Florida Commissioners	Georgia Commissioners	All Commissioners
Yes	26.6	22.3	24.3
No	73.4	77.7	75.7

TABLE A.9
POLITICAL AMBITIONS: LEVEL OF GOVERNMENT
(in percentages)

Level	Florida Commissioners	Georgia Commissioners	All Commissioners
Federal	4.3	0	2.3
State	39.2	28.6	34.1
Local	56.5	71.4	63.6

Appendix B

Questionnaire

THIS questionnaire was mailed to Florida and Georgia county commissioners. The questionnaire to Florida commissioners was mailed from Florida Atlantic University under a cover letter from that institution; the questionnaire to Georgia commissioners was mailed from the University of Georgia under a cover letter from that institution.

Dear Commissioner:

The Institute of Behavioral Research at Florida Atlantic University is conducting a study on some selected aspects of county governments in Florida. This study is aimed at an objective assessment of the involvement of county governments in some important problems currently facing our state. Given the importance of county governments not only to Florida, but to the nation as a whole, this is an endeavor that is vitally needed.

Your cooperation in this venture is urgently needed. The information you provide will be handled and reported on a statistical basis only, and you may feel assured that all responses will be treated in strictest confidence. At the completion of the project in August, 1972, I would be more than pleased to make a copy of the findings available to you. The questions are self-explanatory, and you will have no trouble in answering them. However, if you have any questions about the project, please feel free to write or phone.

For your convenience, a self-addressed envelope has been attached. I am hopeful that you will complete the enclosed questionnaire and return it as soon as possible.

Thank you for your cooperation.

Appendix B

1. In your opinion, what are the two most pressing problems now facing your county?

   a. _____ b. _____

2. Here is a list of problems that your county may now face. Would you please indicate to what degree these are now problems for your county? (If one does not apply, check "not applicable.")

	Severe	Not Very Severe	Not at all Severe	Not Applicable
Financing County Services				
Lack of Business and Industrial Development				
Drainage				
Planning and Zoning				
Welfare				
City Annexation of County Land				
Housing				
Roads				
Public Health Facilities				
Flooding				
Law Enforcement				
Water Supply				
Solid Waste Management				
Droughts				
Sewage Treatment				
Air Pollution				
Recreational Development				
Administration of County Government				
Education				
Busing				
Preserving Open Spaces				
Water Pollution				

APPENDIX B

3. Would you please indicate which level of government you feel should take the principal responsibility for handling and solving these problems. (Check one or more if you see fit).

	City	County	Special District	State	Federal	Others (Write-in)
Financing County Services						
Lack of Business and Industrial Development						
Drainage						
Planning and Zoning						
Welfare						
City Annexation of County Land						
Housing						
Roads						
Public Health Facilities						
Flooding						
Law Enforcement						
Water Supply						
Solid Waste Management						
Droughts						
Sewage Treatment						
Air Pollution						
Recreational Development						
Administration of County Government						
Education						
Busing						
Preserving Open Spaces						
Water Pollution						

4. Here is a list of water problems your county may now face. Would you please indicate to what degree these are now problems for your county? (If one does not apply to your county, check "not applicable").

	Severe	Not Very Severe	Not at all Severe	Not Applicable
Water Supply for Agriculture				
Water Supply for Domestic Purposes				
Water Supply for Industry				
Water Supply for Recreation				
Water Supply for Fish and Wildlife				
Water Supply for Salinity Control				
Pollution from Domestic Sewage				
Pollution from Industrial Waste				
Pollution from Agricultural Waste				
Flooding				
Drainage				
Beach Erosion				
Salt Water Intrusion				

5. Would you please indicate which level of government you feel should take the principal responsibility for handling and solving these water problems. (Check one or more as you see fit).

	City	County	Special District	State	Federal	Others (write-in)
Water Supply for Agriculture						
Water Supply for Domestic Purposes						
Water Supply for Industry						
Water Supply for Recreation						
Water Supply for Fish and Wildlife						
Water Supply for Salinity Control						
Pollution from Domestic Sewage						
Pollution from Industrial Waste						
Pollution from Agricultural Waste						
Flooding						
Drainage						
Beach Erosion						
Salt Water Intrusion						

6. How effective do you think each of the following measures might be in dealing with any water use problems your county might face?

	Very Effective	Fairly Effective	Not Very Effective	Not at all Effective
Water Rationing				
Flood Plain Zoning				
Control Population Growth				
Desalting				
Land Use Planning				
River Basin Planning				
Regional Planning				
Weather Modification (e.g., Cloud Seeding)				
Interbasin Transfer of Water				
Higher Water and Sewer Rates				

7. How much do the following measures hinder or contribute to land use management in your county?

	Hinder	Contribute
Zoning Practices		
Building Code Practices		
Subdivision Practices		

8. We would now like to get some indication of what activities a county commissioner's job entails. On the problems listed on the left-hand side of the page, would you indicate if you engage in any of the job activities listed across the top, by placing a check in the appropriate blank. If you <u>do not</u> engage in a job activity for a particular problem, leave the space blank.

JOB ACTIVITY

PROBLEM	Close Supervision of County Administrators	Actually Take a Hand in County Administrative Matters	Scrutinize What is Recommended by County Administrators	Determine if the County Should Engage in the Activity	Bring the Problem to the Attention of the Commission	Define What the Problem is	Establish What Should be Done with Regard to the Problem
Financing County Services							
Welfare							
Roads							
Solid Waste Management							
Planning and Zoning							
Water Supply							
Law Enforcement							
Recreational Development							

9. On these same problems, we would now like to know how frequently you deal with public officials in other units of government. If you frequently deal with the public officials listed across the top, please indicate by placing a check in the appropriate space. If you infrequently deal with these public officials, please indicate by leaving the appropriate space blank.

PUBLIC OFFICIALS

PROBLEM	City Councilmen in your County	City Administrators	Special District Administrators	County Commissioners in other Counties	State Legislators Generally	County's State Legislative Delegation	State Administrators	Federal Administrators	Congressmen
Financing County Services									
Welfare									
Roads									
Solid Waste Management									
Planning and Zoning									
Water Supply									
Law Enforcement									
Recreational Development									

10. We hear a great deal these days about growth and development. Here is a list of
statements about activities on growth and development. Would you tell us if you
generally agree or disagree?

	Agree	Tend to Agree	Tend to Disagree	Disagree
"We should promote county growth and development"				
"We should encourage statewide control of county growth and development"				
"We should seek cooperation with adjoining counties in planning for county growth and development"				
"We should allow private landowners to use their land as they see fit for growth and development"				
"We should stabilize current county growth and development"				
"We should provide more services to our citizens as a means of encouraging more people to live here"				
"We should utilize stricter zoning practices to limit county growth and development"				

11. There seems to be an ever increasing demand for county services. Here is a list of
some strategies for dealing with the costs of county services that might be necessary
in the future. Please indicate now much you generally agree or disagree with these
strategies.

	Agree	Tend to Agree	Tend to Disagree	Disagree
"Increase Property Tax Rates"				
"Increase non-property tax and revenue sources (e.g., licenses, fees, fines, users charges,etc)"				
"Assess property more closely to market values to increase property tax base"				
"Get more aid from the federal government through grants-in-aid"				
"attract more valuable industrial (not commercial) property to the community"				
"attract more valuable commercial (not industrial) property to the community"				
"Use zoning, building codes and subdivision controls to regulate the influx of residents who require higher levels of service"				
"Increase resources through federal revenue sharing"				

12. In facing future demands for county services, there may be some activities that you feel your county should or should not engage in. Here are some statements about county activities. How much do you generally agree or disagree with them?

	Agree	Tend to Agree	Tend to Disagree	Disagree
"Counties should expand their services just as cities are doing"				
"Counties should not hesitate to increase their debts to finance projects if they cannot otherwise be paid for"				
"Where possible, counties should set aside land for large-scale industrial development"				
"Every county should provide in its budget for amenities such as parks, libraries, etc."				
"Counties should utilize strong land control policies to shape the direction of its growth"				
"Counties should live within their financial means"				

13. Now, we would like to ask you some questions concerning how issues that are brought before the commissioners are handled.

	Very Often	Often	Not Very Often	Never
How often do the commissioners vote unanimously on issues that are considered?				
When the commissioners are in disagreement on an issue, how often do the same commissioners vote together?				

14. On what kinds of issues do the commissioners most likely vote unanimously? Please list not more than three if possible.

a._____   b. _____   c. _____

On what kinds of issues do the commissioners most likely split their votes? Please list no more than three, if possible.

a. _____   b. _____   c. _____

15. Now, we should like to ask you about the amount of work being a commissioner involves. For each of the following questions, please check one of the categories.

	More than 300 days per year	200-299 days per year	100-199 days per year	99 or less days per year
Approximately, how many <u>days</u> do you spend the <u>whole</u> day on commission work?				
Approximately, how many <u>days</u> do you spend only <u>part</u> of the day on commission work?				

16. If possible, please indicate the <u>one</u> issue that seems to cause the most contact by citizens, groups, and interests in your county.

_____

17. With respect to this issue, which single community group or interest seems to contact you the most?

_____

18. How often do individuals affiliated with the following groups contact you as a county commissioner?

	Never	Not Very Often	Often	Very Often
Agriculture Interests				
Developers				
Real Estate Interests				
Conservationists				
Municipal Leaders				
Citizens Groups				
Other Government Officials				
Labor Unions				

19. Looking toward the future, what <u>one</u> county-wide improvement, in your opinion, does your county need most to be attractive to its citizens?

_____

To complete our survey, we would appreciate your answering the following questions as fully as possible.

1. Where were you born? _____   _____   _____
                                    City   County   State

2. In what year? _____

3. How would you describe the place where you presently live?

    City___   Suburb___   Small Town___   Rural Area___   On a Farm___

4. How many years have you lived here (in your county)? _____
                                                          Years

5. What is your occupation?

    _____
                        description of actual work

    IF RETIRED, PLEASE INDICATE WHAT YOU DID BEFORE RETIREMENT AND CHECK HERE ( )

    _____

6. What was the last grade of school you completed? (Check one)

                    Less than high school   _____
                    High School (graduate)   _____
                    College Incomplete   _____
                    College Complete   _____
                    College (graduate work)   _____
                    Trade School   _____

7. Which of these rough income categories do you belong to?

                    Less than $5,000   _____
                    $5,000-$9,999   _____
                    $10,000-$14,999   _____
                    $15,000-$19,999   _____
                    $20,000-$24,999   _____
                    $25,000 and over   _____

8. What church do you belong to?

    Protestant _____   Catholic _____   Jewish _____
                name of denomination

    Others _____   No Affiliation _____
            please name

8. What local civic organizations, if any, do you belong to?

    _____   _____
    _____   _____

9. What professional organizations, if any, do you belong to?

    _____   _____
    _____   _____

10. Do you usually think of yourself as a Republican, a Democrat, an Independent, or what?

    Republican _____   Democrat _____   Independent _____

    Other _____   (Please specify) _____

11. And, how do you register in state or federal elections? As a Republican, a Democrat, or Independent?

    Republican_____   Democrat _____   Independent _____

12. How long have you been a county commissioner?

    Years _____   Which Years? From _____ to _____

13. Have you held any other public offices?

    Yes ( )   No ( )

    If yes, what were they? (1) _____(2)_____(3)_____

14. Do you plan to seek any other public offices?

    Yes ( )   No ( )

    If yes, which office(s)? (1) _____(2)_____(3)_____

    ADDITIONAL COMMENTS: